Frank Rawlins is a former journalist born in
Lincolnshire, England, and now living near Oxford.
He edited two provincial newspapers before
becoming a freelance writer and editor. Some years
later he realised an ambition by venturing into garden
design. He combined the two enterprises for a while,
until the gardener was overcome by a resurgent
writing bug.

SIMPLE MATTER OF STYLE

Frank Rawlins

Huck Books

Published in 2013 by Huck Books,
Oxfordshire, England

ISBN 978-1483921600

www.huckbooks.co.uk

I am indebted to all those who helped me improve my craft, especially the late Frank Law, who took the young Frank R under his wise and waggish wing.

My thanks also to Struan Robertson, Lawrence Webb, Terry Sutton, and Sue Baron for their valuable advice and suggestions for the following three little primers, now combined into one book.

L *for*

LITERATURE

**A little
primer
for new
writers**

Take the first step to a new skill or maybe
a new career, from journalist to novelist

Frank Rawlins

INTRODUCTION

Anyone can be a writer. In the same way that anyone can be a footballer. Or a dancer. Or a chicken sexer (it is legal – look it up).

I think I'll stick with the football analogy: it will be less tense and messy all round.

I had a sports-mad father and two older footie-mad brothers. As soon as I was toddling steadily enough to stay upright for more than twenty seconds, one of them would be kicking a ball to me. I soon learned to kick it back – after the damned thing had stopped. Eventually, as I grew, I learned to trap or stop the ball dead in its tracks. To kick it, with some degree of control and accuracy, with the inside of my right foot, then the outside. And then with my left foot. To toe-poke the ball. Then to hit it full belt with the meat of the foot – to put the laces through it, as they say in the trade.

My Mum, by contrast, on the few occasions she was cajoled into beach football, would take a swing with her right foot, miss the ball completely, and the unaccustomed momentum of the ascending limb would dump her on her bum on the beach. It was painful to watch. But funny.

A lifetime at the David Beckham Academy, had there been such a thing in her lifetime, might have got her to the miss-but-stay-upright stage.

So right here, before we've barely met, I have to say I might not be able to teach you anything at all.

But the fact that you've taken the trouble to acquire this little primer indicates you have the most important quality a new writer needs – the desire to do it, and to do it to a reasonable standard.

Okay? Good.

Bringing the football analogy round full circle, my Mum went through the early-twentieth century version of British state education: the basic three Rs (four if you count Religion) until her early teens when she went into service.

But she wrote a nice little letter, did my mother. In the main, simple words and plain construction – the basic trap and kick. But occasionally flowering to take in a word with a Z that she usually miskicked and wrote with an X. For instance, *'He's craxy, if you ask me.'* But she didn't fall on her arse; I knew what she meant.

So … her little boy learned how to do it reasonably well. And then along came Pele and Best and Cruyff, Banks and Moore, Charlton and Law, Eusébio, and later Beckham and Ronaldo and Messi. Or, as I progressed through two very good schools, that analogous team of Kipling and Wilde and Twain, Dahl and Dickens and Nabokov, MacLean and Spillane, Fleming and Wodehouse, with – who else? – Shakespeare at centre-forward.

What a team. This person who purports to show you a thing or two about the basics of writing would give his second-best keyboard to be that good. And yet …

I went through the paper mill. I learned the hard way. I paid my dues with a proper apprenticeship. The sort of apprenticeship that a few years earlier, while I was barely a teenager, took a promising little Scouse band to Hamburg, where they played and played and played for a pittance. To an ever more appreciative audience. It stood them in good stead – they came back home to the UK and became the unstoppable Beetroots.

No, I am not comparing myself to the Beechnuts. I am just saying that, unlike most 'reality TV talent show' performers of today, the Bees-knees and I paid our dues. We did it for a paying audience. And they didn't ask for their money back.

I joined my local newspaper at 19 after my A-levels (didn't fancy university; couldn't afford *not* to work) in the days when local newspapers hired just enough staff to train juniors properly – by the simple expedient of paying them a pittance. And ours had an old-style stickler for an editor. Get it right (names, addresses, ages, titles, you name it) – or your testicles are in severe danger. It took two years and a proficiency exam to get me up to standard, and for my gonads to relax.

I moved on and became good enough to be deemed subeditor material. I was given other reporters' work to fit into a page; to mould and to improve; to make the most of every word when editorial space was at a premium. Even if it was just a filler, a one-paragraph story, towards the bottom of a page.

Make it fit, make it correct, make it *very* readable.

Forgive the own-trumpet-blowing, but I became a pretty good subeditor. Then chief subeditor of an evening paper, and finally an editor, before making a dash for freedom and freelancing.

I spent much of the latter stages on the then new free newspapers, when free newspapers had a reasonable story count, excellent stories, and some style (a few still do). But as the novelty wore off and advertising revenues dipped, staffing levels took a concomitant hit. Raw newcomers were the order of the day, be they (increasingly) graduates or school leavers.

Their letters and their CVs were okay; their essay/treatise or general writing *appeared* okay. But let them loose in the real world, and some – particularly the graduates, it seemed – could barely string a handful of words together, let alone a couple of clauses. (So come on, you editors of today, give bright school-leavers a chance!)

The newspaper group I worked for as a freelance didn't have a style guide, so I set to work compiling one – bit by bit, as time and temper dictated – to give newcomers a starting point of what was expected and what wasn't expected. And that's where I intend to start right now, with you: a slightly updated version of the guide starting with the 'technicalities' of compiling a news story for a middle-of-the-road provincial newspaper, and occasionally dotted through with authentic professional jargon, 'translated' only where the meaning isn't obvious.

You might not want to be a reporter but most of

the do's and don'ts apply to all writing to some extent, I believe. They are basic building blocks that will hopefully instil a measure of confidence and discipline, standing you in good stead wherever your writing takes you. I will try to present them as simply as possible; not once will I try to explain the gerund or the predicate (you're right – I've forgotten). But as long as we all know the basics of noun, verb, adjective, and so on, all will be well.

Rules are there to be broken, of course, but if you feel you have a good reason to break them, break them with style and preferably a little humour.

But rules also exist for a reason – in this case they make reading easier and more enjoyable. And that's two pretty good reasons for getting it right.

One final note before I launch into the style guide part of my little primer: I hope all English-speaking-and-writing people can enjoy and benefit from my experience, but I haven't the time, or at the moment the will, to translate some of the words, spellings, and assorted language differences into American English.

I'm sure any American readers will have more than enough intelligence to translate it for themselves.

For those who haven't, I would just say … by football, I mean soccer.

Okay, buddy – let's go.

Oh – sorry, one other thing. Some of my prejudices and pet hates will shine through occasionally.

Yes, all subeditors are part-time pedants – it goes

with the get-it-right ethos – but there is generally a good reason for it. In my case, it's because I hate political correctness, bureaucratic stupidity, most political and business jargon, celebrity culture and so-called reality television, ever-more media dumbing-down, careless pundits, flimflammery, and …

You'll see.

A LITTLE GLOSSARY

There is some UK newspaper jargon in the following pages. None ventures into the arcane realms of em and en, stone and slug, so most examples are generally simple to understand. Even, in some cases, in general use. But, just in case, these are some you will come across:

Caps – capital letters

Dog's cock – slang for exclamation mark, thanks to the shape of the canine doodah, or indeed of a fully engorged exclamation mark. (It's more often known in the trade these days as a 'screamer', but, hey, what sort of imagery is that?)

Intro – first paragraph of a story

Lead – main story on a page

Lower case – small letters, as opposed to capitals

Par – paragraph

Quote – The words said by somebody quoted in a story, OR – a quotation mark

Splash – main story on the front page.

Typo – typographical error (also known in the trade as a literal).

TIPS FOR CONSTRUCTING A NEWS STORY

THE TECHNICALITIES

Intros should generally be short (15-25 words) and confined to the main point of the story. Stick to roughly this length of sentence for the rest of your news stories.

If you have the ability to write longer sentences that flow and read well, do so – but only if you are writing a feature.

The second paragraph should contain the second most important point of the story; the third paragraph, the third most important point; and so on. This means that subeditors up against a deadline and with limited space to fill can, if need be, cut a story just by lopping it from the end.

In general, confine page leads to 200-300 words. Secondary stories should be 100-150. Fillers should be just that – one or occasionally two paragraphs long with a tasty kernel.

Some leads, by their very nature, must be longer. The splash could be considerably longer, or split into two. But keep them as tight as possible by avoiding repetition, by using only the relevant parts of quotes, and by ensuring the quotes don't dribble on.

(L for Literature note: Word count will vary considerably from newspaper to newspaper, depending on space available. Space was at a premium in this instance.)

KIPLING AND HIS COHORTS

Yes, it's hackneyed but true – most stories should answer five questions a reader might reasonably ask. They are the five Ws: Who? What? When? Where? and Why? There are some fillers that won't need all that information cramming into them; there are some circumstances (reporting juvenile crime, for instance) where we are unable to reveal them all.

Go one better by adding How? and you have Mr Kipling's 'six honest serving men'. No? Look it up.

FACTS AND FIGURES

Got a lot to answer for, has old Rudyard. All those names, ages, addresses, jobs, events, towns, titles have to go in. But whatever you do, do not load them into one or two pars. The brain cannot take in all the different facts if thrown at it in one chunk. Bring in names and jobs, ages and addresses bit by bit in succeeding paragraphs.

AND THEN THERE'S 'AND'

'And' is a perfectly good word, and can be effective when starting a sentence. But many lazy reporters just shove it in as a 'joining' word because they have neither the wit nor the inclination to think about a better way of writing. This is a recent example:

The fire at Headington Cricket Club on Barton Road was attended by Oxfordshire Fire Service, and it is thought the fire was lit by youths using petrol who were seen at the premises earlier in the evening.

This is crap writing. It wouldn't be quite so crap if

it was split into two sentences:

The fire at Headington Cricket Club on Barton Road was attended by Oxfordshire Fire Service. It is thought the fire was lit by youths using petrol who were seen at the premises earlier in the evening.

But then again …

THINK ABOUT WHAT YOU'RE WRITING

For example, the above sentences should have gone something like this:

The fire at Headington Cricket Club on Barton Road was thought to have been started by youths – seen there earlier – using petrol.

(Of course it was attended by Oxfordshire Fire Service – it was in Oxfordshire!)

ONE SENTENCE, ONE THOUGHT

On a similar theme, remember that a sentence is basically about one thought/idea/action. Take this common mistake:

Hayley said: "There was a great party at Jan's, some posh ginger-haired chap called Harry chatted me up all night."

Despite the apparent link of party and chat-up, this is two thoughts/two actions, and thus should be two sentences; or at the very least one with a dash or semicolon in the middle:

Hayley said: "There was a great party at Jan's. Some posh ginger-haired chap called Harry chatted me up all night."

Or –

Hayley said: "There was a great party at Jan's –
some posh ginger-haired chap ..."

Or –

Hayley said: "There was a great party at Jan's;
some posh ginger-haired chap ..."

However, semicolons don't sit comfortably in most news stories, particularly in quotes, so go for the dash.

And don't let Hayley go to any more posh parties.

ONE INVERTED SENTENCE, TWO ALTERNATIVES

Keep things simple, and the right way round. For some inexplicable reason, lots of people can't stop themselves writing backward sentences like this: *In the council's recent Local Plan, a business park and a hotel have been included at the site.*

This is much neater and easier to read: *The council's recent Local Plan includes a business park and a hotel on the site.*

Or –

A business park and a hotel are included in the council's recent Local Plan for the site.

*(**L for Literature** note: This doesn't necessarily apply to other forms of writing, such as the novel – but it takes practice to get an inversion that is natural and seamless.)*

PUNCTUATION IN GENERAL

If in doubt, remind yourself of the purpose of each punctuation mark.

A full stop calls a halt to each particular thought or idea or action.

A comma is a slight pause in the thought or idea or action.

A colon is used where a second clause elaborates on the first:

There was one good reason why he was considered the world's best second-hand car salesman: he was taught by David Cameron.

It is also used before a quote:

George said: "Tell you what, Tony – let's bomb Iraq."

A semicolon is used where a different but related thought or idea or action is introduced:

The junior minister is quite mad; the Prime Minister promoted him only last week.

Don't be afraid of short sentences. A good read mixes in short and longer sentences.

QUOTES

Good quotes (not just any old quotes) bring a story to life, especially if it is a dramatic story, an action story, or even a funny story. But make sure the quotes reflect that drama/action/fun.

And don't let them dribble on till they become boring or meaningless.

STARTING POINT

Can't quite get the intro? Or how the first 3/4 pars should go/develop?

Talk to yourself! (or your screen, or phone, or

someone nearby who isn't too busy).

Try telling the story as you would to someone in the pub, or at home. By long practice and instinct, your brain will get to the gist of the story almost automatically. This may sound stupid – BUT IT WORKS.

TRY IT!

TIME FOR A LITTLE PAUSE

The style guide that follows is but a simple affair that I put together for junior reporters as and when mistakes cropped up.

If you go on to work for a newspaper or newsletter or magazine, your publication may well have an entirely different style guide. It could be a volume in its own right; it could offer different solutions to common difficulties, depending on the nature of its content and its readers.

In the UK all the major national and provincial newspapers have their own guides, most going into the intricacies of modern life – whether certain celebrities spell their first name Alistair or Alastair, the use or otherwise of the apostrophe in Homer Simpson's *D'oh!*, or the pros and cons of using roman numerals in a story.

They do it because uniformity is important. Readers get irritated if you can't make up your mind between queueing and queuing, between Koran and Quran or Qu'ran.

However, the need for the definitive spelling of Gabriel Márquez Garcia rarely crops up in local newspapers, so I stuck to the basics: common mistakes, regular misspellings and misuse of words; stuff that has a grizzled old editor grizzling till his hair falls out. It's also stuff that will benefit any new or would-be writer.

I should add that lesser sticklers, would-be writers

or otherwise, might find some of the edicts a mite old-fashioned. Outdated even. In some cases it's hard to disagree with the heretics. Language lives and evolves, and we are probably fighting a losing battle. But … for me it's a matter of standards. Like good manners, let them slip and the new lesser manners become the norm. And none of us wants that.

DO WE!?

Okay. But for those lesser sticklers who wouldn't know a slipping standard if it told them where to eff off, I have highlighted a few – the ones you really ought to try to help me save – by inserting the initials LBW. Which, American readers might be grateful to know, is nothing to do with the arcane laws of cricket. They stand for Losing Battle Warriors, of course.

Right.

Read, enjoy, and try to remember. Read again, enjoy again, and you will remember. Promise.

USAGE (of words, language, punctuation) – IN OUR STYLE

A or An BEFORE H?

An before a silent H (*an* hour); *a* before a sounded H (*a* hotel). In other words, pretty much as you say it (unless you're one of those shudder-inducers who *always* sound the H – see **AND FINALLY ...**).

ABBREVIATIONS

Do not use full points: Mr, Mrs, mph, BBC, NHS. Spell out rarely used acronyms the first time: i.e. Bicester And Launton Lapdancing Society, followed by ... um ... or you could just call it the society. But i.e., as you have just noticed (haven't you?), takes full points because it looks seriously odd without them.

AFFECT OR EFFECT

This explanation may *e*ffect a change, or perhaps have no *e*ffect. Both with an *e*. Your reaction will certainly have an *a*ffect on me. With an *a*. None the wiser? Rewrite the sentence! There are whole books without either word. Or you could just ask around.

AFTER/WHEN/AS/WHILE

Be careful how you use common linking words (prepositions), such as *after* and *when*. Most are NOT interchangeable, so think first. For example:

The soldier was injured after a sniper shot him from a nearby rooftop.

Injured *after*? Pardon? Did something else happen *after* he was shot? Did a piano fall on him from a third-floor window? No? In that case, it should read:

*The soldier was injured **when** a sniper shot him from a nearby rooftop.*

ALL-IMPORTANT
Is it really? This annoying little phrase is used to describe anything these days, from the weather forecast to the line-up for England's next match. It might be interesting, but *all-important*? Life, death, love, and family are all-important. The squelchy bits between the last two are quite vital, too.

ALL RIGHT
Always two words. Alright is not all right.

ALSATIAN
An Alsatian with a cap A is a person from Alsace. Or a dog with ideas above its station. Try lower-case *a*lsatian.

AMONG
Not *amongst* (archaic, biblical, and/or lawyer-speak).

AND I? Or ME?
You and I, Terry and I, or Sue and I appear this way when we are the subject of a sentence.

When we cease to be the subject, change it to you and me, Terry and me, or Sue and me. Still not sure? It's easy. Try it without your partner. For instance, if you can't decide between …

He gave the job to Terry and I
He gave the job to Terry and me
… without Terry, it would read
He gave the job to I.

Quite! *Terry and me* is correct. Write anything else and I'll send Tel round to sort you out (he's a 6ft 6ins, 18-stone, baseball-bat-wielding bouncer).

APOSTROPHES

(Not apostrophe's! This would-be plural is only for silly sod's who sell Tomato's and Potato's.)

Apostrophes are really very simple coves. They describe the possessor/owner.

So, **write the possessor first**. For instance, if it's *one* dog:

The dog

and then add the apostrophe and the s:

The dog's bone.

Thus we know it is *one dog with one bone*.

*

If it is *more than one dog*, write the possessors first:

The dogs

and then add the apostrophe:

The dogs' bones.

Thus we know it is *more than one dog with more than one bone*.

*

Be wary of plural words that don't end in an s:

Not womens' rights, or childrens' toys

But women's rights, or children's toys.

*

If the possessor ends in an s, such as Charles, it is strictly speaking correct to write the possessive as Charles's, as in Charles's crown, but Charles' crown is easier and accepted nowadays. Use the latter.

*

APOSTROPHE IN IT'S

The only time *it's* has an apostrophe is when it is short for *'it is'* or *'it has'*. Thus:

It's time to go home.

It's been a nice day.

Oddly, in the possessive, there is no apostrophe. Thus: The dog ate *its* bone.

*

AND FINALLY ON APOSTROPHES:

There are no such words as *her's* or *their's*.

BIBLE

Use a capital if you're talking about *the* Bible. Lower case if you say, "The Beer Drinker's Guide is my bible." Always lower case for biblical. But Koran and Koranic both take a capital K.

BILLION

It always used to be a million million in the UK, but now we've come into line with the US it's a thousand million. That's inflation for you.

BOUGHT and BROUGHT

Fifty lashes for anyone who mixes them up (including the otherwise erudite TV gardener who has a blind spot). Bought is the past tense of buy. Brought with an *r* is the past tense of bring also with an *r*. Easy to *r*emember.

'C' OR 'S'

(L for Literature note: American readers should, of course, ignore this entry)

Practice, licence, and advice *with a 'c' are nouns* (his advice was to obtain a licence to allow more practice).

Practise, license, and advise *with an 's' are verbs* (he advised me to license the firm and practise more).

'C' OR 'Z'

Recognise, organise, demonise, please. Leave the z variations to the good old UZ of A.

CAPITALS

Do not cap up people's job titles: managing director, editor, and so on.

Do cap up official bodies: Cherwell District Council

Do not cap up council committees: Cherwell District Council housing committee

Do cap up 'official' words that also have a general meaning:

The Chancellor unveiled the *Budget*

BUT The editorial *budget* is somewhat tight

The latest *Act* to go through the Commons

BUT An *act* of revenge

Do cap up *EACH* word of titles of books, films,

plays, and so on:

One Flew Over The Cuckoo's Nest (*Not:* One Flew *o*ver *t*he Cuckoo's Nest).

The same goes for organisations.

This example shows why: ... *on behalf of Ellen Kent and Opera International.*

Is this on behalf of a person and a company? No, Ellen Kent And Opera International is the name of a single production company.

CHAIRMAN
(LBW ALERT!)

Is always correct. As is chair*woman*, if you prefer. But never use chair*person* or *chair* ... that is something you sit on. Why succumb to this political correctness, when 'man' is patently used in the sense of humankind and not of some big hairy thing with sticky-out genitals.

CLICHÉS

Avoid them like any contagious bacterial disease characterised by fever and delirium. Or use them when only a pithy phrase will do and you haven't the time to come up with a new cliché.

Seriously ... whenever you find yourself writing a cliché, and we all do, just stop and think for a few seconds. Either try another form of wording, or try to tweak the cliché.

For example:

Geoff used to drink like a fish.

How about changing it to something like (but

using your own imagination):

Geoff used to drink like an AA reject.

It's well worth a few seconds' thought.

COMMAS
(AND PARTICULARLY THE SO-CALLED OXFORD COMMA)

If you haven't heard of it, the 'Oxford comma' is the extra comma that the vast majority of people, and thus writers, don't bother with. It is the comma that scholars and, some say, pedants like to use before the word 'and' in any list of more than two items:

I ate fish, chips, mushy peas, and bread.

Most people prefer:

I ate fish, chips, mushy peas and bread.

Well … I am no scholar, although I confess readily to professional pedantry, but the OXFORD COMMA IS CORRECT USAGE. So there!

The anti-Oxford movement comes unstuck when a list can be ambiguous, as in:

The train will stop at Bicester, then Haddenham and Thame.

That is not three stations; Haddenham and Thame is the name of the station after Bicester.

It gets even worse with:

The train will stop at Bicester, Haddenham and Thame and Princes Risborough.

Anyone unfamiliar with the area and its railway won't know (UNLESS YOU USE THE OXFORD COMMA) whether there are four stations, or three with one called Haddenham and Thame, or three with one called Thame and Princes Risborough.

The correct form is:

The train will stop at Bicester, Haddenham and Thame, and Princes Risborough.

So, generally speaking, it is best to use a final comma in any list longer than two items.

It is equally important to use the final comma in a list of actions. Look how ridiculous this is:

For exercise Mark liked to lift weights, swim and skate at Oxford Ice Rink.

Pardon? Has the ice melted?

This is better:

For exercise Mark liked to lift weights, swim, and skate at Oxford Ice Rink.

This is better still (taking away the ambiguity of how many sports you can do at the ice rink):

For exercise Mark liked to skate at Oxford Ice Rink, lift weights, and swim.

(See also semicolons)

*

ANOTHER COMMA YOU MUSTN'T MISS

I'd like to cook that, Delia

means something rather different from

I'd like to cook that Delia.

Some national publications regularly miss this vital comma. Don't copy them!

*

WHEN TO AVOID COMMAS

He praised every Leicester City fan who lined the streets to greet the FA Cup winners – correct.

He praised every Leicester City fan, who lined the

streets to greet the FA Cup winners – incorrect. Unless every single City fan was there (and I wasn't, for a start). In this instance, *who lined the streets* is not a subordinate clause; it is an adjectival phrase.

COMMENCE
Awful 'official' word – use *begin* or *start*. As for commencement … would you prefer the rack or the ducking stool?

COMPARE WITH
Always use *compare with* for a comparison, as in: *Compared with Goofy, Cheryl is a good singer.*

Compare *to* means to liken to, as in:

I used to compare Simon Cowell to Voldemort, but that's not fair on Voldemort.

CRITERIA
This is plural; the singular is criterion.

CURB
Control or restrain. Only in America does it also mean kerb (the bit Brits hit when parking the car).

DATES
July 25, not July 25th, or even 25th of July
Date punctuation: Monday December 31, 2012.

DIFFERENT/SIMILAR
Different *from*; but similar *to*.
Easy way to remember: if it's different it's going

away from the thing it isn't being likened to; something similar is veering *to*wards it.

DIPHTHERIA
With two *H*s; not diptheria.

DISINTERESTED
Means objective or unbiased. Uninterested means not taking an interest.

DOG'S COCK!
Okay in headlines but generally to be avoided in stories. Use only with genuine interjections or exclamations, as in: *"Rubbish!" shouted the editor.*

It is tempting to use an exclamation mark to tell readers where they should laugh. Don't!

*(**L for Literature** note: Journalists tend to get the veto drummed into them, but many authors do not. Journalists who go on to become authors tend to let the dog's cock creep back in. Myself included. Idiot!)*

ENORMITY
(LBW ALERT!)
Refers to something bad or abominable, not huge. Enormousness represents its size. Not a word that trips off the tongue – so try magnitude or immensity. Or change the sentence to use enormous as an adjective.

EVERYDAY
Means ordinary, mundane. Every day (two words) means every day.

EXTERMINATE EGGS-TERMINATE!

The next person to write an intro or headline on an Easter story using any made-up word beginning with eggs- (as in *eggs-cellent, eggs-traordinary*) will be exiled. See how easy it is to resist.

FINAL E AS IN BLONDE

The word *blonde* with an 'e' describes a female. A fair-haired male is *blond*. This applies to both noun and adjective.

Similarly, *fiancee* is female; *fiance* is male.

All from the French. Bien sûr.

FLAMMABLE

And inflammable mean the same thing – easily set on fire. The opposite is non-flammable.

FORENSIC

(LBW ALERT!)

The proper, original meaning of the word is 'relating to a court or legal matters'. Thus, people who investigate scenes of crime are not forensic experts; they are *forensic science experts* or *forensic scientists*.

GAFFE

A mistake. A gaff without the *e* is the hooked implement anglers use to land fish. Or a cockney house.

GRANDDAD

(LBW ALERT!)

If gran*d*ma and gran*d*son keep the *d* on gran*d* then

so should gran*d*dad. No one writes grandaughter – so why is grandad acceptable? Tosh! Double d in the middle, please.

HARASS
Just the one *r*.

HEADLINES
Master the art of writing a good story first – then we'll talk headlines.

HER MAJESTY or
HER ROYAL HIGHNESS
Sorry, we're not at court now. Do not use! The Queen … will suffice.

HOARD and HORDE
Hoard with an *a* is an *a*ccumulation of goodies. Horde with an *e* is an *e*normous number of people.

HYPHENS
Use hyphens in adjectival phrases such as *the come-right-in welcomers* (a nifty coinage from an absorbing travel book by some former journo). Do NOT use a hyphen when the first word is an adverb: for instance, the phrase *hastily arranged meeting* does NOT take a hyphen between the first two words.

ICON
(LBW ALERT!)
An icon is a religious painting, not a building, a

bridge, a film star, a footballer, a book, a TV programme, or anything else that is the flavour of the month. Angela Merkel is NOT an icon; she's not even an oil painting. Maggie Smith comes close, though.

INCIDENT

Do not parrot this 'official' word. It is a pathetically weak word that British police forces have successfully infiltrated into the newsroom and everyday life, superficially to allay public fears but in reality to defuse press coverage and assuage their civic 'partners'.

Police use it in every press statement, whether written or spoken. It is used to describe road accidents, murders, riots, rapes, you name it.

When they say, *'Police are seeking a man after a vicar was found dead with a knife wound in his church. The incident is believed to have happened ...blah blah blah ...'* PARDON?

THE INCIDENT?

CHANGE IT!

The *murder* in the nave (not the incident)

The *pile-up* on the M1 (not the incident)

The *rape* on the common (not the incident).

All forms of media have succumbed to the incident syndrome. DON'T LET THEM GET AWAY WITH IT! Tell it like it is.

*(**L for Literature** note: When someone is charged, the murder becomes the alleged murder, but this isn't the place to examine press reporting restrictions. See LIBEL towards the end).*

INVARIABLE, INVARIABLY

Means *always, never changing*. It does NOT mean changing occasionally or sometimes.

INFINITIVES

Feel free to split them when it sounds right.

'To go boldly where no man has ...' just doesn't have the same impact.

LAST/PAST

If you are reporting the forthcoming Armageddon, use last:

The *last* five years of the world ...

Otherwise, use past:

The *past* five years of famine ...

LEAD/LED

The past tense of the verb lead is *led*; not lead – this is a metal.

LESS IS FEWER, SOMETIMES

Less is the adjective for a singular object, as in:

I earn *less* money now than ...

Fewer is the adjective for plurals:

I work *fewer* hours than ...

LITERALLY

Don't use it – unless you know *precisely* how to use it. I once heard a TV sports commentator say: "Triple jumpers literally turn into human kangaroos." He meant, of course, metaphorically. Amazingly, at the time of writing, he is still working.

LOATHE, LOTH
Loathe – hate, detest
Loth – unwilling, reluctant
(L for Literature note: Some writers might prefer loath for unwilling, but the loth variation distinguishes the words more easily.)

LOSE
It is becoming a common mistake to spell lose with an extra 'o'. DON'T DO IT!
You *lose* something if it is misplaced; you *loose* (or *loosen*) something that is too tight.

MINISCULE?
No such word – try min*u*scule.

NONE
Strictly speaking, it takes a singular verb, as in:
None of us wants a bonus.
But the plural often sounds better, as in:
None of the bankers have voted against a bonus.

NO ONE
Is two words (no hyphen). Nobody is one word.

NUMBERS
One to nine are spelled out; 10 onwards are in figures. But do *not* start a sentence with a figure:
Twenty blackbirds were found in a pie today.

*(**L for Literature** note: In my books I have reverted to spelling out most numbers, except very large ones, as the discerning among you may have noticed.)*

NUMBERS/VOLUME

Amount is by volume or mass. Therefore ...

A great *amount* of people is no doubt a pile of about three tons' worth.

The correct word is ... a great *number* of people.

ONE IN ...

One is singular. Therefore, One in 10 people *has* ...

NOT One in 10 people *have* ...

ONLY

I used to be a bit of a pedant about this little word. Strictly speaking, it should be placed next to the thing it is qualifying, as in:

"*I eat only fish on Fridays,*" *said the Catholic traditionalist* (because he refused to eat meat on Fridays).

Whereas: "*I only eat fish on Fridays*" was the norm for a Protestant friend who couldn't bear the thought of fish on Monday to Thursday or the weekend.

So, strictly speaking again, the following sentence should read: *She died only two days ago.*

But the version that goes *She only died two days ago* reads more naturally, so don't be afraid to loosen your stays and use it.

OVER

Indicates a position above, or resting on the surface of. So for figures, this is correct:

More than 700 asylum seekers ...

PEOPLE/THINGS

People are people, not objects, so *DO NOT* say:
The vets *that* appear on the telly ...
The people *that* write for newspapers are ...
(or, worse still, The people *which* write ...)
Those *that* can't write ...

The correct versions are:
The vets *who* appear on the telly ...
The people *who* write for newspapers are ...
Those *who* can't write ...

POST-MORTEM

(LBW ALERT!)

This means literally 'after death'. Therefore to say '*a post-mortem revealed*' is nonsense.

It is correct to say: *A post-mortem examination* (or report) *revealed ...*

PUNS

Fine if they are clever and original, and are used in light-hearted stories. Otherwise ... DON'T DO IT!

QUOTATION MARKS

Inverted commas, usually referred to in the newsroom simply as 'quotes'.

Always use double quotes (with single quotes inside if needed):

Dolly Parton said: "I will always remember the costume fitter's first words, 'Bang goes the budget'."

Note sequence of final punctuation: close single quote, full point, close double quote.

(L for Literature note: Most novels use the single quote format, with double quotes for subsidiary clauses. I have followed the trend with my books. It feels right somehow. But readers soon adjust to those authors who prefer the double quote.)

QUOTES

As a rule, gct in the name of the speaker first (to identify him or her immediately) and use a colon:

New coach Roy Boy said: "I'm sure I can improve the England team ..."

Use the name at the end where the speaker has already been identified:

"It was a freak goal," said Mr Boy.

Note positioning of full point in the following examples:

Whole quote – *He said: "Sod off, you reporters."* (point inside quote mark)

Part quote – *He said that Mr So-and-so was "a raving prat".* (point after quote).

When using a long quote, split it into more than one paragraph; start each par with a quote mark, but only put a close-quote on the final par.

(L for Literature note: Most novels use the comma, rather than a colon, after naming the speaker: Mr Thingy said, 'Blah blah ...'. *It tends to look better in a book.)*

RESTAURATEUR

Not restaura*n*teur. There is no *n* in the word because of some obscure French declension that I won't bore you with.

Could I but remember it.

REVEREND

Generally speaking, this should be used as an adjective, always preceded by 'the':

The Reverend John Wot was the finest preacher ...

After the first use, revert to Mr/Mrs/Ms:

Mr Wot added...

Where possible, refer to an Anglican priest as vicar (usually a rural parish) or rector (urban parish).

Avoid using The Reverend as a title, thus:

The Reverend said in his sermon ...

SAID or SAYS?

'Said' is nearly always best with any quote:

*"Got some strange names, these Brits," **said** Newt.*

If you are writing a feature in the present tense, 'says' is just about acceptable:

*American politics is still a mystery to most Britons. "There's a lot of name calling," **says** Mitt.*

Never use the verb first:

***Said** Bear Grylls: "I'll stick to wildlife presenting."*

The correct way is:

*The Americans both **said**: "Grills? Bare Grills?"*

SEMICOLONS

Usually commas will suffice in a list of actions or things. But if you must use semicolons, once you have embarked, keep going.

DO NOT miss the last one, whether it is a list of actions:

Peter's regular jobs included: ranting at all and sundry; parking his car and reparking it several times; going to the shop round the corner for a variety of nuts and pulses and asking for a rise for all the juniors.

Wonder what the shop assistant thought about his last request. It should, of course, be:

Peter's regular jobs included: ranting at all and sundry; parking his car and reparking it several times; going to the shop round the corner for a variety of nuts and pulses; and asking for a rise for all the juniors.

Or a list of things:

The plans for revitalising the town centre feature: a new multi-storey car-park with a bowling alley on top; a new 37-screen cinema; a tree-lined avenue named after Gideon George and the world's largest sewage system.

The mind boggles. It should, of course, be:

The plans for revitalising the town centre feature: a new multi-storey car-park with a bowling alley on top; a new 37-screen cinema; a tree-lined avenue named after Gideon George; and the world's largest sewage system.

Got it? Good.

SINGULAR OR PLURAL?

Beware of inadvertently mixing the two. It's easily done, but also easily avoided. Take this sentence, for example:

*If you have **a** good subeditor, you are in luck. **They** will see the best in your work, as well as the faults.*

A good subeditor, followed by *they* ... Uh?

There's a simple solution that, for some reason, people either don't see or seem afraid of using:

*If you have **a** good subeditor, you are in luck. **He or she** will see the best in your work, as well as the faults.*

Give it a go.

SINGULAR OR PLURAL
COLLECTIVE NOUNS

Companies, councils, schools, and most other bodies are singular:

The council *has* agreed ...

And watch out for:

The council *has* agreed that *their* budget ... (the second italic word should be *its*).

Teams, bands, and police are treated as plurals:

Oxford United have been relegated ...

Oasis are playing the Kassam Stadium ...

The police were investigating ...

With other collective nouns, decide if the group of people is acting as one unit or a gathering of individuals. Hence:

The news team is improving by the day.

BUT ... *The news team were busy buying coffees.*

THAT OR WHICH

They are not always interchangeable.

That tends to define. For example: *The car **that** took us to Stamford was a battered old jalopy.* This assumes that we already know about the trip to Stamford; the clause defines the nature of the car.

Which tends to inform. For example: *The car, **which** took us to Stamford, was a battered old jalopy.* This assumes we know nothing yet; it informs us about the car and where it took us.

TILL

Correct, less formal and friendlier version of UNTIL. Never use *'til* – this is for people who write *BBQ* instead of *barbecue*.

TIMES

At 8pm, not 8.00pm. And definitely not 8pm *in the evening* (pm is always evening).

Eight o'clock at night is okay, if a mite long-winded.

At noon, or at midnight; but *not* 12 noon (noon is always at 12).

TOP

Avoid this lazy catch-all word when you mean leading, senior, eminent, important, expert, and so on. Is the Pope really just a top Catholic?

TRY TO

The verb try should be followed by 'to'.
'Try and' is incorrect.

If you think this is pedantic, try it in the past tense:
*He tried **to** write the perfect sentence* – correct.
*He tried **and** write the perfect sentence* – UHH!?

WHILE
NOT *whilst*, unless writing to a lawyer.

WHISKY
For the Scottish variety, but whisk*e*y with an *e* for the Irish (or US) version.

WHO or WHOM
Tricky cove, but basically it depends on whether your *who/whom* is the subject of the clause:
*He kissed the most buxom model, **who** he thought was the prettiest in the show*
Or the object of the clause:
*He kissed the most buxom model, **whom** the rest derided for her tarty look*s.
However … *whom* is fast disappearing in speech so if in doubt use *who*.

WINDSCREEN
Not windowscreen!

XMAS
Too awful for words. Christmas, please.

Y ENDINGS/PLURALS
For those words that end with a consonant followed by a *y*, change to *ies*:

Lorry, lorries
Story, stories
For words that end with an *ey*, just add an *s*:
Journey, journeys
Storey, storeys

AND FINALLY...

Nothing to do with writing, but everything to do with setting a good impression when speaking to your contacts or readers:

The word 'aitch' has no aitch when spoken.

Thus, when you say something such as 'HMS Ark Royal ...'

You pronounce the initials 'Aitch Em Ess'

NOT '*H*aitch Em Ess'.

Don't do it!

*(**L for Literature note**: I have heard several BBC presenters passing on this calumny to a generation that will speak as it's told. Sadly, some teachers do it, too. Who among you parents out there has the guts to correct them?)*

YEAH, BUT WHAT ABOUT 'CREATIVE WRITING'?

Okay, so you don't want to be a reporter. You want the freedom to write what you want to write. Not what some idiot news editor tells you to write.

You want to write an epic that flows and flowers like some sylvan stream. Or explodes off the page like a best-selling thriller. No? You want to write a sitcom; a sitcom so funny no one dares read it for fear of dying of convulsive laughter. Or perhaps you want to write a satirical blog so withering that politicians will shrink in its wake, or your growing band of followers will tweet the world.

Or maybe you just want to write a nice long letter to your Mum. You craxy old thing.

Whichever ... how do you begin?

As of today, I have published six books, four of them novels. Actually, I have written one and a bit more novels than that: the first one was reasonably well written but didn't quite gel somehow; the second I just ran out of steam, proving that it wasn't a great idea in the first place. But they did show me how to start and finish a novel.

First, make sure you are writing something that will fire your imagination and keep it fired. If you just go through the motions ... well, readers can generally spot crap.

So, idea first. Well, I can't tell you how to dredge

up the great best-selling idea. That's entirely down to you and your brain. Obviously, heed the old maxim – write about what you know. But equally obviously, use your imagination. Let it run to places it's never run before.

So, idea settled. There are basically two ways to approach writing your novel, and both are relatively straightforward.

THE PLOT

1. Plot your book in close detail before you begin the long slog. Work out your story line, from the first sentence to the last. Settle your characters – from names to underwear preference – and the way you want them to interact. Work out each turn and byway of the plot.

2. Determine the starting point and finish of your great idea. Fix your main characters in your mind. Conjure up an engrossing first sentence/paragraph. And then, like life, let your writing take you where it will, from motorway to country lane, from chasm to blue sky, from lover to unpredictable stranger. You will surprise yourself, and therefore your reader. YOU WILL BE ORIGINAL!

Of course, you can be original with either method. But I suspect that most would-be literary adventurers will find the second option easier, and therefore most suitable. I certainly do. But it's all down to temperament and discipline. As with the actual writing, follow your instincts.

So, that's the plotting sorted.

THE WRITING

Make your first sentence, first paragraph, first chapter the best in the book. Then make your second chapter the best in the book, and so on.

Okay, so that sounds facile; impossible perhaps. But it's an aim you must always bear in mind, or your work may fade to mediocrity.

I have found the best way to try to achieve the impossible is to revise as I go along. Don't leave your revision to the end – you might find you have to rewrite the whole bloody thing, and that's probably enough to kill most literary ambition.

When I'm writing in earnest (I practise every day, be it just an email or perhaps the latest stonking MyBeboFaceSpaceTweetBlog...thingy), I start the day by revising what I have written the previous day. I read it mainly for flow and sense, to see if it still grips me (and therefore my imaginary readers), or to see if I find my eyes glazing over and my ancient brain wondering what's for lunch.

If something doesn't work, doesn't flow or gel with the rest of the narrative, I work at it until I think it does. Sometimes just one paragraph from the day before can take an hour or more to sort out and that's very frustrating because I want to crack on. But persevere I do. If it's one of those brain-freezers I will call up a new Word page and try different versions until I get the one that at that moment seems exactly right. If I get really stuck, I will pull a sheet of A4 out of the printer and write it in ink in longhand.

That's desperate. But necessary.

When I have finally finished my early revision – realising I have also corrected typos and maybe minor style or syntax misdemeanours along the way – I begin today's slog.

It may seem slightly excessive, but I also do a fairly quick revise at lunchtime after a three(ish)-hour morning stint, mainly for typos, badly chosen words, and so on. I usually also revise my afternoon session before knocking off for the day; again mainly for easily spotted mistakes.

As you progress, your revising should take up less time most mornings, before you plunge once more into the unknown.

And there's another tricky cove …

DISCIPLINE

It's the writer's great predicament – finding a new start point every day. Many is the day your brain won't just come up with one. It's the everyday form of writer's block. The sniffle or cold, compared with pneumonia. But you can fight your way through it.

Read your last few paragraphs again. Do the next few paragraphs follow on? Or is this the place for a new section, a new chapter even?

Just try something – anything – on that new Word page, or sheet of A4. Okay, so you've just written a load of rubbish. Scrap it – write some slightly less rubbishy rubbish. Oh, look – there's a hint of a good sentence, an idea, even a tiny gem hiding under the dross. Let's just try …

KEEP TRYING!

If you don't keep trying, you will have wasted a day.

I know – it's hard.

One of my favourite writers, Douglas Adams, had a chronic 'getting started' problem. Legend has it that his publisher had to lock him into a hotel room as deadlines approached and barely a thing was written, releasing him only for supervised walks. He once said, "I love deadlines. I love the whooshing noise they make as they go by."

I have but a fraction of Douglas's natural talent, but I wallop him on the discipline front.

You can do it, too. And you'll find it much easier to start each day if you revise the previous day's output first.

THE BIG FINISH

If I am anything to go by, you will get a strange feeling as you near the end of your book. It's elation, and yet ...

The final couple of chapters are seemingly taking for ever. You thought it would be all over in a day or two, and you're tempted to just chop it there. But no. Persevere. And still the day or two turns into a week. Maybe a week and a day ...

There's a great temptation to cut back on the revising; an even greater temptation just to rattle off the first vaguely appropriate words that spring to mind.

Be patient. Stick to your daily routine. The end will come.

And so will your final read-through.

THE FINAL REVISE

A book can always be improved, but as with an artist who finds it difficult to stop tweaking a colour here, a shadow there, there comes a time when you have to accept that this is your best draft – any more and you are in danger of losing the spontaneous and the spark. The flash of inspiration that made you realise spontaneous can sound good as a noun, whereas spontaneity would drain the sentence of any, well … spontaneity.

This book is finished – you have another to start planning and writing.

I find it's best to revise your own book again, from start to finish, before anyone else sees it. But, if you can, leave it for a few weeks. It will come back to you at least semi-fresh. You won't remember every line; you won't subconsciously skate over sentences lodged in your brain and engraved on the back of your eyeballs.

Look for anything and everything. Typos, inadvertent name changes, non-sequiturs, possible libels (a soupçon more of which later), unwanted changes caused by a careless mouse. And, of course, passages that make you nod and smile, jokes that make you laugh, passages that have you blinking away the tears – yeah, you've done a good job.

If you are lucky enough to have a good publisher, you will probably get a good editor too. He or she will see your work with fresh eyes and a professional touch. He or she will see the spontaneous and the spark; the typos you have missed (and there will be some, no matter how meticulous you think you are); the odd syntax or punctuation problem.

If you have to go the self-publishing route – a route that I welcome and embrace, and a route that has already thrown up many fine writers – make sure you have some bright and amenable friends (or be prepared to pay for professional readers/editors).

You need two or three intelligent people; people who are well-educated, literate, book readers, book lovers, meticulous, honest, reliable. Long-suffering, too, obviously.

Proper friends, in other words. They'll need to be when you ask them to read it (please) for sense and enjoyment. Make a note (please) of typos or other mistakes. Could they say (please) if there are sections in the book they don't like, and why; and bits they do like, and why. And any other comments they care to make will be gratefully received.

When they eventually report back – please be patient – you may have to re-evaluate things. The chances are they will like or dislike different things. Try to be dispassionate as you weigh their reasons. It's no good asking people to read your book and then ignoring their views if they don't like something. These are you readers – some of your paying readers may be thinking similar things. So ...

Think how you could incorporate useful suggestions without ripping up the book and starting again. Some minor tweaking may well do it.

It is worth it. In my first (published) novel I gave one of the characters a new lease of life, thanks to one suggestion. And in my later Peru 'holidaylogue' I followed another suggestion that made a significant difference to the overall reading enjoyment, as ebook sales have proved.

Thank you, friends.

And Mrs R, of course.

THE IMPORTANT OTHER BITS

READ READ READ

I must admit I don't read enough. I'm too busy writing during the day, and I tend to watch TV or attempt a Sudoku or crossword in the evening. But at bedtime I do settle down with a paperback (or Kindle) and my beloved. Before too long, however, I'm either asleep or a-cuddle. Or both. Either way, not enough reading gets done.

Going back to my football analogy, reading Twain or Dickens will not necessarily make you a better writer any more than watching Ronaldo or Rooney will make you a better footballer. But here physical limitations don't come into play. You can assimilate hints and acquire good habits almost by osmosis. Or, if nothing else, you will get a feeling for good writing.

Incidentally, I'm not just talking books here. There are some fine writers on newspapers and magazines across the UK and America. Europe too, I'm sure, could I but understand them.

And if you want to be a journalist, get into the habit of reading as many newspapers as you can – it's part of the job. I used to read the opposition papers and at least one of the national newspapers every day. I used to read so many back then that these days I just buy one big fat bugger on a Sunday and read it bit by bit over the week.

It's plenty when you've spent half a lifetime at it – I'm excused boots now.

TRY TO FLY

Don't be hidebound by convention, by advice, by rules suggested by crazy people who write crazy books on how to write sensible prose. In other words, let your own style develop.

Don't be afraid to try new things, to bypass the cliché, to connect certain words so well they might become a new cliché, or to invent new words even. Don't be afraid of those longer sentences that editors and newspapers ask you to eschew. Practise often enough and you might well find yourself soaring off to new heights, taking your readers with you to a new place, a new discovery, so wondrous they will be lost to the mundane world, and not even realise they have just read a sentence, a perfectly understandable sentence, of 60-plus words with nary a semicolon to help the breathing. If you can't, don't worry. Keep 'em short.

Practise enough and you could soon be ignoring the basic sentence rule of 'subject, verb, object' and splitting it into dynamic sections. One or two key thoughts. Thoughts, like the previous sentence, that might not need a verb.

It's all about practice and confidence.

Don't beat yourself up with the intricacies of ambiguous punctuation. Yes, get it right, but there are places where there may be two rights, and they don't necessarily make a wrong.

You probably didn't notice that in the preceding pages I have written:

You can do it, too.

Followed by:

If you are lucky enough to have a good publisher, you will probably get a good editor too.

Yes, you can use the word too in this 'also' sense (as opposed to the 'overly' adverb sense) with or without the comma. In my view, the first example looks right with it; the second looks right without it.

So there. You didn't even spot it; it must be all right.

LIBEL

Libel is a complicated business – that's one of the reasons why lawyers are so rich. Libel laws also vary from country to country, although most are based on the old English laws of defamation.

Writers of fiction are unlikely to be troubled by libel, although it can happen in rare circumstances. So if you are having a scurrilous dig at someone, make your characters vague/different enough from reality to leave enough doubt.

Writers of newspapers and other news media have subeditors, editors, and retained lawyers to keep them out of trouble. But it is always wise to remember that the truth is a complete justification in law. Fair comment is also a proper defence for the media: think mean-minded critics slagging off a play so viciously that it closes after one night. If it's the critic's honestly held opinion then all is well, for the critic at least.

Other defences in the UK include qualified and absolute privilege, which mostly deal with the right of scurrilous politicians to say just what they like in parliament.

Libel payouts can be horrendous, so never be tempted to cross the line. If you are, check with a lawyer before succumbing to the temptation.

AND FINALLY ...

So, your precious manuscript is finished to your satisfaction, or as close to it as you can get without being driven to dementia. That is the hard bit over. But there are many more pains and pitfalls to conquer before your book is published, be it on paper or screen.

This is not the place to go into the intricacies of publishing, either conventional publishing or self-publishing. The ascent of the latter, taking a growing slice of the market from the former, means it is ever more difficult for the unpublished writer to acquire an established publisher. Try it, by all means, but meanwhile, while your manuscript waits on the slush pile, learn to format it as an ebook.

It should be fairly straightforward but it never is. If you can afford it, you can get a specialist formatter to do it for you, but having got this far, the satisfaction of doing it all yourself is immense. The same goes for the cover.

Try not to get too frustrated or impatient. It all takes time.

But you have taken the first step.

You are a writer of books.

Yes, you are.

You may not be the Messi of literature. But then can Messi defend? Stanley Matthews (no? – ask your grand*d*dad) couldn't run quickly if his house was on fire, but the baggy-shorted Blackpool winger could waltz round defenders as if they weren't there. Ronaldo can strut and preen, but can he do modesty?

We all have our own talents. Practice will hone your strengths.

UNLESS ...

Still too daunted for words?

Newspapers are in some ways a lot easier. But then again, there's more than just the writing. There's the art of interviewing; learning shorthand (yes, it's still a requirement, at least in the UK, and it's damned hard getting up to the required 100 words a minute); the best ways to build up a good Contacts Book; the ability to schmooze; the laws, other than libel, that affect journalists, such as contempt and privacy; the required capacity for booze.

These, however, are topics for a different time and place. This little primer is just about the basics of literature, in its original sense: written works. Not necessarily highbrow and definitely not highfalutin. But, hopefully, always readable.

Whichever way you swing – good luck!

AND MY FINAL 'FINALLY' …
WRITE WRITE WRITE

I achieved a degree of footballing competence by practising. Whenever and wherever there was a ball to be kicked, I kicked it.

It's all very well being coached by some joker with a keyboard and a couple of books to his name, but the real skill, the real finesse, comes from within. The joker can give you the pointers: the tips, the do's and don'ts. But …

YOU have to bring it out. YOU have to coax it and develop it. YOU have to nurture it.

And, unless you're that rare thing, a genius, the only way to do that is to kick your words around as often as possible. Every day if possible. Even if it's just an email, a memo.

Better still, when you get some spare time, use it to write a few paragraphs about an everyday incident (out, damned word!) and make it as interesting as you can. So that someone else reading it won't stop after the first five words, but will nod his or her head, or smile.

In other words, pay your dues. Even if you don't yet have a paying audience. You have to put in the work.

I still do. Admittedly, with an eye to using my everyday you-know-what in some future book, but that's because I've spent most of my life making a living from words.

Try it. Keep trying it.

Here's a little bonus (I hope) to show you what I mean:

The first and so far only (and undeniably lovely) Mrs R and I had a day out to see Windsor Castle. The spring weather was fair, the joint mood was congenial, and we had a terrific day trip; the sort of day trip that makes you wonder why you bother with proper holidays.

I had nothing on the next day, so I thought I'd write 'A quickie in Windsor' piece just in case I need the wordage for my next 'holidaylogue'; when I eventually get round to writing *A Lifetime Of Holidays ... Part Two.*

It turned out all right.

So I thought I would show you first how it might have turned out in guidebook-speak. But then I couldn't bring myself to do it. I can't write like that because my years of practice won't let me subject my readers to something so boring they will be weighing up the proposed House Of Lords reform after the first paragraph. So then I thought ... I'll just demonstrate, hopefully, how a few simple events can be turned into something readable.

And that's my final and my best tip: Make a barn door interesting from one yard and you're a proper writer.

See what you think:

Near-perfect day out

The strangest thing happened as my wife and I drove into Windsor, looking for signs for Parking and the Castle that had been marking our route for miles but disappeared just when we needed them.

With traffic in front and behind beginning to con-certina, I made a sudden decision to turn off into a quiet residential street and ask somebody for direct-ions. It was all posh parking bays and dotted white lines with warning notices about Parking Permits, a Queen's Ransom for a ticket from a machine hidden from view, or the Death Penalty.

A well-groomed fortysomething woman was stand-ing behind a formidable 4x4 vehicle in the nearest bay looking down at its gargantuan spare tyre on the tarmac. As I hove to and got out of my trespassing car she started taking pictures of the tyre with a digital camera.

I asked politely for directions to the nearest car park for Castle visitors.

She replied politely, in a charming Irish brogue, extolling the virtues of the car park back the way we had come – turn left at the lights, straight on, and then right – dismissing the nearer multi-storey as ridicul-ously expensive.

Then, looking momentarily back down at her ob-viously recalcitrant tyre, she suddenly said in an even more charming brogue, 'I've had a terrible run of bad luck lately. I'm going to be a Good Samaritan and see if that changes things. I'll fetch you a Parking Permit. You can park right there all day for nothing, and the Castle's only a few minutes' walk away.'

She smiled with a sudden relief, as if these two unknown day trippers had freed her from some Faustian shackles, and dashed into the nearest house, to return half a minute later with our permit.

I was going to ask her about her run of bad luck, and whether the huge tyre had anything to do with it, but she skipped back inside with an even bigger smile.

We had definitely done her a favour …

Calling all incontinent entrepreneurs! While I'm in munificent mood, let me bring a wry smile to your anguished faces. If the little café on the corner of the crossroads nearest the Castle ever comes on the market, snap it up and you'll look on your affliction with affection.

Like all savvy sixtysomethings, we rarely pass up the chance of a wazz, so Joy and I decided to pop into the café for a coffee and a wee (thus preparing ourselves for the next coffee and wee in the daily viscous circle, and that's not a typo) before embarking on the Castle Trail, because these places are often light on loos.

Being polite Brits, we ordered the coffee first and then asked where the lavatory was.

'Sorry, but we haven't got a toilet here,' said the aproned assistant with a smile that said to her boss 'Caught another one, Gwen!', and directed us to the public loo just twenty or thirty yards down the street.

Having started our expedition with such Gaelic serendipity, I resisted the urge to ask whether it wasn't compulsory for cafes to offer a lavatory. Instead, I guarded our seats and cappuccinos while Joy toddled off first, and within half a minute three Americans came in, ordered coffee, and asked where the bathroom was. They also had trouble believing our Provision Of Facilities In Public Refreshment Establishments Act, but restricted their chagrin to shaking heads and rueful smiles that said 'Goddam, Limeys – don't they kill you'.

Anyway, on to the Castle and a lengthy security procedure that would have pleased any of the monarchs, from William the Conqueror onwards, who used Windsor as a hideaway from trouble. And Charles after he married Camilla.

The long queue in front of us – and this was well before high season – consisted largely of Americans, Japanese, Chinese, and our Commonwealth cousins, but with a healthy smattering of Brits finally keeping promises to themselves to 'do' Windsor Castle one day.

And, for all of you who haven't yet done it, it is worth doing. It's magnificent, from the first walk up towards the Round Tower, where I stopped more than once to say in an overloud voice, while pointing upwards and pointedly ignoring the foreign hordes shuffling past us, 'That's the room where I stayed last time.'

We wandered down to the parade ground in the

Lower Ward just in time to see the Changing Of The Guard; and then to tire of the various hiatuses interrupted only by an occasional military stamping of hobnailed boots, shouldering of arms, and blowing of bagpipes.

We went back up the hill towards the State Apartments. And what a royal trove of treasures we discovered. Rubens, Rembrandt, Bellini, Bruegel, and, for the Americans, Dick Van Dyke are all there within the first few chambers – the King's Bedchamber, the Queen's Audience Chamber, the Queen's Presence Chamber, to name but three.

Then there are the vast tapestries, the incredible sumptuous ceilings no doubt inspired by substances Shelley would have given his false teeth for, the precious china, the rare military hardware, the mighty chandeliers, the marble, the statues, the busts, the gold and silver, the whole incredible wealth and opulence of this strange wonderland revered throughout the world as the British monarchy.

Then comes the room that Joy, like every female visitor, from child to granny, wanted to see more than any other: the room housing Queen Mary's Dolls' House. It is the opulent dream in miniature, from the rich interiors with their running water and electricity, to the little garden designed by horticultural guru Gertrude Jekyll, to the 14cm-high wind-up gramophone complete with vinyl records of *God Save The King* and *Rule Britannia*, to tiny books with real printing inside, but nothing from Huck Books.

Our visit coincided with a photographic exhibition

for the Queen's Diamond Jubilee, featuring some stunning shots of HM, and some with members of the Family Firm, that interested even a royal sceptic (have a guess).

And then we were back out in the fresh air. To discover with some pleasure that there was now a long queue for the State Apartments (those souls who couldn't drag themselves away from the Eventual Changing Of The Guard) and no queue for the nearby loos for our first royal wee.

I won't meander on much longer – this isn't a free advert, Charles – because, like us, you must now be almost knackered.

The secret is, for all you oldies, not to use the audio commentary thingy – you'll be there forever. We both took one at the first stop after Security but immediately noticed how long it was taking people to get around. The only time we used it was when we made our final stop at St George's Chapel, back down in the Lower Ward.

The Chapel is something special, even for a religious sceptic (still no prizes). The stone fan-vaulted ceiling, the work of humble artisans, is fine art at its most sublime, up there (literally in this case) with the Old Masters.

The facts and figures coming through the headphones were too many to take in, so we finished our visit by buying an excellent official guide book for a fiver – and that is a free advert – to browse at our leisure.

And so back into the only slightly less rarefied air of Windsor town. We had an excellent 'free lunch' at Café Rouge, courtesy of some Tesco vouchers, I bought a £45 shirt reduced to £20 in the sale at Fat Face, Joy found some bargain earrings at Monsoon, and when we arrived back at our car, fearing a practical joke and a wheel-clamp, we discovered it wasn't a dream.

We had had a near-perfect day out.

Lovely.

Thank you, Irish lady, for setting it off – hope your luck changed.

GOOD SPOT!

Eagle-eyed journalist will have spotted, of course, as they arrive at the end of part one of *Simple Matter Of Style,* that I haven't been entirely consistent in my use of quotation marks. But then again ... maybe I have.

I have stuck to what I know and what is generally accepted as best practice – double quotation marks where the reported speech will appear in a newspaper, and single quotation marks where it is for a book.

Carry on ...

'Good grief! It's funnier than the first one!'
Guardian (no, not that one)

B *for*

Part 2 of the little
primer for new writers

babble, bafflegab, balderdash,
baloney, bamboozle, banal,
befuddle, bilge, black arts,
bombast, bookish, bored,
bowdlerise, brainy, bravura,
Braxton Hicks contractions,
brazen, breathless, brevity,
Brobdingnagian, and ...

BROCA'S AREA

Frank Rawlins

<u>INTRODUCTION</u>

Okay, so after reading *L for Literature* you've been practising your writing skills every day. Yes? Well, most days. Now and again?

Good. Me, too. And I hereby lay the proof before you, after a few words of explanation.

I concluded the first part of my little primer with a cameo of a visit my wife and I made to Windsor Castle in May.

The day trip was so good we returned in November, using the same tickets ... but fortunately no one threatened us with the Tower.

It was the Queen and Prince Phil masks that did it.

I jest, of course. On your first visit you just ask a warden to stamp your ticket and it converts into a one-year pass. Bargain, eh.

So, anyway, here's the second part of the Windsor saga:

Not a bad day out

It was the sort of autumn day that would have had Franz Kafka drooling – damp round the edges, puddles clogged with fallen leaves along the road to the M40, a hint of fog threatening to make the motorway a nightmare.

Traffic was heavy and slow, and we went through one foggy section near High Wycombe – some say it's there even in high summer – but otherwise it was plain snailing (and I hereby patent that new cliché).

This time, instead of dicing with the parking gods, I had downloaded a route from the internet taking us from our front door to a convenient car park close to the Castle.

'20 Vacancies' said the electronic sign.

'That'll do nicely,' said I.

I drove past the first vacant bay because it was an awkward titchy gap and I didn't feel like motoring gymnastics – and discovered that the electronic sign should have said '1 vacancy'.

We did a lap back to the single space and found another car squeezing in.

Bugger!

We wanted to see the Semi State Apartments, which had been closed in May. *Semi?* I thought they were more splendid than the State Apartments. Particularly the Crimson Drawing Room, which is very crimson but even more gold; the State Dining Room, which the Queen still uses for entertaining guests (and we're still waiting for the invite); and views of the Castle Garden that are unavailable from anywhere else on the visitor route.

We eschewed the headphone commentary entirely this time, and discovered that asking one of the many wardens keeping an eye on proceedings was so much more satisfying. For both parties. The two we asked positively delighted in breaking from their silent, standing, watching brief. And we loved the nuances that a machine and a script can never bring to an explanation.

If you make the journey, ask the chap in the Grand Reception Room about the huge malachite urn presented to Queen Victoria by Tsar Nicholas 1 in 1839. And learn how it did a striptease in the great fire of 1992 but was subsequently restored to respectability. Great stuff.

We did St George's Chapel again, because it's such a wonderful place and because we needed a sit-down (on fold-up seats in lieu of proper pews) for a while. And then we hit the town.

We wandered down the little side street just off the entrance to the Castle, and discovered the Nell Gwynn Chinese Restaurant. Yes, we did a double-take, too.

Apparently the building was the home at one time of the actress who was the mistress of King Charles II and possibly a lover of King Prawns Szechuan Style. We just wanted a snack so we strolled on to an Irish pub on the corner, had some unexceptional Elizabeth II chicken wraps, and then did a little shop browsing.

No bargains this time; just very tired legs. So we moseyed on back to the car and headed for our five-mile sojourn on the M4. We were reflecting on whether Nell was a rice or noodles sort of wench when we arrived at what appeared to be the world's busiest and most intricate roundabout. But instead of going round it again, as I normally do when the navigator and I have a route to check out (our record is nine times round and a spat that lasted almost as many hours), I headed for the A-road that would link us with the M40 and home. Only to find ourselves in almost-rush-hour traffic snailing through Slough.

Bugger again!

The good news is that Slough isn't as big as we feared. Before long I was on a road I knew from my freelance days and we were back home to watch the end of *Countdown*.

So, all in all, our return trip to Windsor was ... Vowel Consonant. OK?

MORE INTRODUCTION

The first thing you will have noticed, of course, is that this practice piece is roughly half the length of Windsor Part One. And you will have undoubtedly twigged that this is because it makes sense to distil any sort of writing down to the readable essence. To the interesting, the quirky, the funny, the whimsical even, as long as it's engaging whimsy. Otherwise your reader will soon turn to another writer.

I came across this example of travel writing not so long ago ...

You can sit on this part of the beach for hours without getting disturbed. Just take in the views, although it's a bit flat and samey, or go to sleep. There are ice cream sellers near the town end and that's where families tend to gather. There are no donkeys either end of the beach although there were some years ago. There are still some deckchairs, although they don't look very sturdy.

... And was just about to nod off when I thought of you and the next tip.

Don't write without thinking; don't write just for the word count. Don't write just for the sake of writing; write for the sake of improving if it's practice, and if it's not practice, write for the sake of informing, engrossing, amusing. Or whatever is your aim.

To revert to my footballing analogy in *L for Literature*, there is little point in kicking a ball against a wall and having to turn round and fetch it time after time. You kick it against the wall so you can hopefully, eventually, learn to master its movement: by trapping it, by volleying, by half-volleying, by flipping it up and smashing it with the outside of your foot.

Right ... so what is the best way to practise writing?

I touched on it last time. I'll develop it now.

BROCA'S AREA

In simple terms, Broca's Area is the region of the brain responsible for the *production* of language. It was named after the French neurosurgeon Pierre Paul Broca who discovered its function in the years from 1861 when he began to examine the brains of deceased patients who had had speech difficulties.

And what is writing but speech set down, be it on paper or screen. It might be flowery, it might be rough and ready, it might be streetwise, it might be comic, but most literate people could speak it with some degree of confidence.

But when it's the other way round … strange things happen. Even to bright, otherwise intelligent people.

There are business executives who can hold a room with a powerful speech, but put a biro in their hand and their Broca's Area goes berserk. I have known managers who can barely string two written words together. Suddenly their brains become full of officialdom and obfuscation, of antiquated, awkward words; punctuation becomes either non-existent or epidemic; natural rhythm becomes a lame thing that trips, falls, and shatters its kneecaps. It would take a Dench or a Branagh to speak it with any degree of fluency.

So what is the answer? ***Talk to yourself!*** Speak it first. Out loud if you prefer, if there's no one else around, or if you're a raving exhibitionist. Then aim to reproduce it, sentence by sentence, pretty much as you said it. If you speak reasonably well, you will have the basis of a good sentence. Then you can work on it.

My Broca's Area isn't developed enough to come up immediately with sentences such as *'Suddenly their brains become full of officialdom and obfuscation, of antiquated, awkward words; punctuation becomes either non-existent or epidemic; natural rhythm becomes a lame thing that trips, falls, and shatters its kneecaps. It would take a Dench or a Branagh to speak it with any degree of fluency'.*

But it did come up with something like *'Suddenly their brains become full of official, or antiquated, or awkward words. The punctuation is all over the place, so nothing flows. It would take an Olivier to speak it with any degree of fluency'.*

I thought about it for a little while and then started to type, fairly steadily, the words going through my head, had a Broca Moment, and started to elaborate a little. Went for a better mental picture. Chucked out the late Laurence Olivier (because he may be unknown to some younger readers) in favour of Judy Dench and Kenneth Branagh (who will still be well known for several more generations). Finished. Read it through. Added a nifty phrase. Et voila.

Of course, there is always the danger that if you actually write the thing twice, as above, you might decide the original shorter version is better – crisper, more direct, easier to absorb. But then, on third thoughts, the reworked version gives a much better picture of the crippled writing limping painfully along the wrong road.

So … don't get bogged down. Make a decision and stick with it. If you remember from *L for Literature,* at the end of each writing session you will read and possibly revise what you have just written. And at the start of the next working day you will read yet again and *definitely* revise any sections that you think can be improved.

I became fully aware of this writerly dysfunction when I joined my local weekly newspaper straight from school as a trainee reporter and discovered that there was a breed that made the lowest of the low – we cub journalists – look good. The village correspondents.

These men and women kept the entire circulation area aware of all the hot news from their little communities – the annual village fete, WI meetings, harvest festival, dog-fouling in the allotments. And, of course, hatches, matches, and dispatches – births, marriages, and deaths.

Some could write reasonably well, some could get by, some could puzzle the greatest cryptic crossword solvers.

When I had got past my first beginner's pieces – writing up wedding reports from the forms sent in by excited couples or their families, and making sense of the weekly farmers' market prices – sometimes the editor would throw over a couple of the worst village reports and tell me to decipher them. But without totally obliterating the unique style that each village had come to recognise, interpret, and love. And certainly without cutting the writers' lineage payment (an old penny or so per line) from pin-money to risible.

It was perhaps the ultimate test, helping to sort out the would-be men from the schoolboys. If you came through it, you would probably make a decent writer.

In these days of the interweb, Faceblogs, and twittering, of smaller budgets and staffs on local newspapers, the village correspondent is in many places merely a memory, but there are a few enclaves where they hang on. I found a few and now, assuming the role of editor, I throw a slightly disguised one to you to decipher. It's not a total disaster but it can be improved by several degrees.

Have a read and then rewrite it, in pencil (just in case I ask you to try again!). If you have the paperback version, you can use the space below it, for future reference. If you have an ebook, either grab some A4 or fork out again for a good old-fashioned paperback and make an old author slightly less curmudgeonly.

Your correspondent from Tiddlewich was taking a few snaps at the village Cricket Club for the Match reports; and suddenly it was obvious a low-flying aircraft was approaching very low, struggling with his monopod your correspondent managed to get 10 or 12 snaps as the Dakota flew overhead.

The noisy Battle of Britain memorial flight Douglas C47 (DC3) Dakota ZA947 clipped the tree tops (probably on route from one of the early summer air displays at either Shuttleworth or Duxford).

Tiddlewich Cricket Club were playing Tonkem at the Bells Close cricket ground beautifully prepared in most attractive surroundings.

Some of the players dashed for the pavillion as the plane flew over the boundary; and then regained height.

Your go:

My go. This is how I might have rewritten it (after certain checks), were I working on the Shuttleworth & Duxford Times:

A Second World War plane clipped the treetops at Tiddlewich cricket ground on Saturday, sending frightened players scurrying for the pavilion.

The Douglas Dakota from the Battle of Britain memorial flight soon regained height, and the village's match against Tonkem continued.

The Times' local correspondent, Teddy Snapper, who was watching the match, managed to snatch this slightly blurred picture of the plane as it flew from its base at RAF Coningsby, Lincolnshire, to a display at Shuttleworth.

(The third paragraph could be cut entirely, or reduced to the flight path details, if the extra space is needed for a more important story.)

As editor, I would have detailed a staff reporter (Teddy was back at his abattoir job) to find out the extra details you see above. But, first, I would have got him or her to phone the RAF and ask what the hell had caused its Douglas C47 (DC3) Dakota ZA947 to frighten the cricketers at Tiddlewich. It might have turned into an even better story (pilot has a heart attack; bored cricket scorer dazzles pilot with laser beam; RAF's secret fuel cutbacks; who knows?). And then I would have got him or her to speak to a couple of the cricketers (was it *very* frightening?; did they cack themselves; that sort of thing).

Before I go any further, I would just point out a few things the alert reporter (in this case, YOU) should have spotted:

*On route should be *en route*.

*Pavilion is spelt with one *'l'* not two.

*The state of the Bells Close cricket ground is irrelevant; unless it is obliterated by a dying military transport plane, obviously.

*Punctuation is very important. In Teddy's first paragraph, the semicolon just stops the drama in its tracks, and the comma after 'very low' should have been a full point. Teddy's struggle with his camera and monopod (a tripod deficient in the leg department) is something else altogether. The semicolon in the final sentence tends to give the impression that it was the scurrying players who regained height after the scare.

How did you do? Did you use your Broca's Area first, saying it to yourself, either silently or aloud, before launching into the rewrite? I hope so.

This combination of reporting techniques is an excellent way for any new writer to improve technique and, eventually, style. So I intend to concentrate for a while on journalistic writing. If you want the freedom of 'creative writing' please bear with me. Because whatever you want to write – be it novels, children's books, film scripts, sitcoms – you have to do the groundwork first before the real you, the inner you, the artist you, starts to flower.

And there's no better way of doing that than in a newsroom.

WERNICKE'S AREA

Everybody's Broca's Area is different, of course. Some are highly developed; some rarely get past adequate. That's what makes the human species so fascinating; and that's what makes writing – doing it and reading it – so absorbing. Nature and nurture have, for example, given us Enid Blyton's reassuring voice and Stephen King's unsettling voice, and never the Twain (or, indeed, Samuel Langhorne Clemens) shall meet.

But Broca is merely half the story.

Let us not forget Carl Wernicke, a German neurologist and psychiatrist who gave his name to the second part of the cerebral cortex linked to speech and language. Ten years after Monsieur Broca began his study, Herr Wernicke discovered the part of the brain responsible for the *understanding* of language.

What neither of them discovered was that far too many people, although they can produce and understand language very well, simply have little or no idea of how to set it down for others to read. I haven't yet stumbled across the part of the brain responsible for this (still awaiting my form from the Freelance Lobotomists Licensing Authority), but when I do, I think some scientific body should call it the Rawlins' Area.

Like the village correspondent, the press release writer can range from pretty good to good-grief-who-wrote-this-shit?, be they representing a national company, a local restaurant, a district council, a drama group, a police force, or PressReleasesRUs.

I'll plunge straight in with another little exercise for you, based on an already slightly altered press release, in the middle of my spectrum, from British Transport Police:

Investigators from British Transport Police (BTP) have released this image of a man they believe holds key information about disruption to services after an emergency cord was pulled on Thursday, 27 September on a train travelling between Manchester Airport and Newcastle Central.

PC Lindsey Lightfoot, investigating the incident, said: "Around 3.35pm, a man who boarded the 15:06 Manchester Airport to Newcastle Central service at Manchester Piccadilly, pulled the emergency cord when the train was at Stalybridge. The train had to be stopped and the guard had to reset the alarm, causing a delay.

"As the train resumed, the man threatened to pull the cord yet again, causing an unscheduled stop at Mossley, where the man alighted from the train alongside a woman."

Billy Vickers, Police Liasion (sic) *Officer said: "Trains are fitted with emergency stop equipment to ensure the safety and security of all passengers. To misuse this equipment is highly irresponsible and inconsiderate to both customers and staff. We are pleased therefore that the British Transport Police are pursuing the individual responsible.*

"First TransPennine Express will always treat safety as our number one priority and will pursue those whose behaviour and actions jeopardises such."

Detectives have made several lines of enquiry, including reviewing CCTV footage and have since identified a man they would like to speak to.

PC Lightfoot added: "The man's behaviour was utterly irresponsible, causing 28 minutes of delays to services by pulling the cord which is intended for use in genuine emergencies.

"If you know the man pictured, or his whereabouts, I would urge you to get in touch."

Yes, when you've finished yawning, I'd like you to rewrite it, please. And here's a useful clue – for most publications, bar *The Line* (the BTP magazine) and, obviously, *Geeks Weekly*, the following space will be enough to accommodate a crisp rewrite.

Very good! I hope. My psychic powers tell me it is possibly not too different from the way a hard-pressed news editor would have passed it on to his subeditors.

> *British Transport Police have issued this picture of a man they believe caused an emergency stop for no reason, endangering and delaying passengers, on Thursday afternoon.*
>
> *The man pulled the emergency cord of the Manchester-Newcastle TransPennine Express at Stalybridge, causing a half-hour delay while the alarm was reset. He then threatened to pull the cord again, causing an unscheduled stop at Mossley, where he and a woman companion got off.*

Sorry, PC Lindsey Lightfoot, but you would be unlikely to get a look-in on my pages unless it was a *very* slow news day (but you have a great name which I must use in a novel some time).

Okay – getting the hang of it?

In this example there is less (or possibly no) need to speak your sentences to yourself. You have the gist of it in front of you. With enough practice you will be able to simply distil the press officer's words to your editor's requirements and your newspaper's style.

Just don't get cocky. Get practice. Get experience.

RAWLINS' AREA

Cocky. Good word. 'Conceited or confident in a bold or cheeky way', says the *Concise Oxford English Dictionary*. Careful confidence is fine, and you build it through practice and experience. Overconfidence and then conceit is the enemy of excellence.

Neither trait figured when I started this project. I was a smidge wary; veering on frightened, in fact. I have done my share of teaching and bringing on young reporters and subeditors in my own environment – in the newsroom. Demonstrating on the job, as it were. Both individually and in groups. But unleashing it on the English-speaking world was something else; especially as I wanted it broader than just the newsroom. Especially as I wanted *any* novice writer, and not just would-be journos, to be able to benefit from my long experience of writing.

I was still worried when *L for Literature* was published. What gave Frank Rawlins the right to pontificate, for god's sake!

But then I sold a few copies, and then a few more, and they're still selling, and my confidence is back where it should be. I know what I'm talking about. Roughly.

So, football analogy, anyone?

I am not going to bog you down with tactics – do this, do that, don't kick the ref – but I am hoping to steep you in the basic skills and give you the confidence to use those skills to best effect. The motivation to keep on writing and improving.

I have been writing professionally now for 45 years, and I like to think I am still improving. Or at least evolving, mellowing into a style that is all my own, a style that is the essential me.

Okay – enough of me. Back to you.

So, the Rawlins' Area.

According to a little-known amateur neurologist and psychiatrist, it is the part of the brain responsible for converting the spoken word into the written word. Let's plunge straight in to it.

You are working on a shoestring evening newspaper, where most people start at 7am, or earlier. There has been a robbery at the supermarket down the road. There were three masked men, all with sawn-off shotguns. Members of staff were locked in a store room, the manager was made to empty a safe stuffed with the previous day's takings, one shot was fired into one ceiling.

Not long after the police arrive, a supermarket customer (also an avid reader of your journal, *The Merton Mercury*) dashes into the newspaper's reception and informs the rather attractive Melanie behind the desk that there's been a shooting at Sainsrose down the road. Melanie deals with a classified ad customer, checks her lipstick, plumps her hair, and then pops her lovely head into the newsroom to relate the drama down the road.

The news editor, who is having a secret affair with Melanie, immediately dials the police press office and at the same time orders the only reporter in the office – YOU! – to get your arse down there and interview anybody involved. And quick.

By the time you arrive, the police are cordoning off the main entrance, ushering customers to one side to ask for witnesses, and generally keeping new-comers and nosy bastards at bay. You casually ask one constable what is happening.

'We're expecting the Queen, Sir,' he says sternly. 'Now go away.'

You suspect sarcasm may be at work here. But there's no time to dwell on it – you spy a double door round a not-quite-hidden corner and know from previous sightings that that is where staff nip out for a smoke. When no one is looking, you duck under the police tape and sneak round the corner. Four thirtysomething women wearing the familiar Sains-rose tabard and one younger man wearing a junior management tie are indeed having a much-needed smoke.

You introduce yourself and ask what is going on as you pull your pad and biro out of a deep pocket.

The gabbiest woman (and it's a close-run thing) is about to launch into her best story ever when Junior Manager reminds her of the head-office directive never to talk to anyone from the press without head-office approval.

The gabbiest woman ignores the little twerp (this is the good old *Mercury*, after all).

"We was almost finished our late shift when these blokes wearing balaclavas with guns, you know, sawn-off, the guns, I mean, burst into the back. Glynnis said she saw them in the freezer aisle putting balaclavas on. Anyway, they told us to freeze, which was, you know, er … ironic, is it? And then two went through to the boss's office while one stood pointing his gun at us. Frightening or what!? Bloody terrifying, actually.

"Then suddenly there was a shot from the office. Nearly crapped myself. Didn't we, Sharon?"

"Speak for yourself," said Sharon nervously.

"Yes, well," continued Gabby. "There was shouting and what sounded like scuffling. We froze all right. Then it was quiet for quite a long time. And then the door opened. The two men came out with three or four bags each – you know, our lovely Bags For Life – crammed with fivers and tenners, twenties, think I saw a fifty on top. The one guarding us waved us into the room. What a mess! Half the ceiling on the floor and on Ronald's desk. That's the manager. He were on the floor, dazed, a huge bruise under one eye. The left, I think. Or was that my left? Anyway, before we knew it all three of them was pushing people into the office with their guns. Nearly all the night staff. It was like the black hole of … California … in there. Then they locked us in and skedaddled.

"We was all silent until we reckoned they must of left the shop. Then we started shouting and screaming for help. Old Herbert, the odd-job man must of heard something, although he's normally as deaf as a … door. And he let us out. Then somebody phoned the police. They were here in, ooh, three, four, five minutes. Ten tops. Frightening or what!?"

And then a constable comes round the corner, spots your notebook, asks your name and address, threatens you with life imprisonment, or at least a dressing down from your editor and his chief constable, unless you hand over the book. But when he realises you're not quite as green as you look, he smiles, and tells you to get the hell out of there.

By the time you get back to the office, having briefed *Mercury* photographer Harry to get a picture of Gabby (the one with the flying buttress spectacles) and her full name and address, so you can send her a copy of the picture, naturally, your love-struck but hard-nosed news editor has a police press release hot from the old-fashioned fax machine.

It says:

> **There was a robbery incident at Sainrose's supermarket in Grubb Street, Merton this morning (Wednesday the 7th November).**
>
> **It is believed that three men were involved. All were believed to be wearing balaclava-like headgear. At least two were armed, with what were described as shotguns.**
>
> **It is believed one shot was fired, but no casualties were reported.**
>
> **Oxfordshire Police are asking for customers, who were in the supermarket at the time, to come forward, unless they spoke to police officers at the scene.**
>
> **Chief Inspector John Whately said: "The Oxfordshire Police were on the scene within less**

than 10 minutes of the men leaving the supermarket. It is believed they made their escape in a black Peugeot.

"The Force would like to reassure the general public that this type of incident is extremely rare, and they should not be afraid to go about their daily lives as usual."

Contact 01865 ... blah blah blah.

Your first edition deadline is roughly half an hour away. So get writing! Combine the press release with what Gabby told you.

I won't leave a blank this time (on the off chance that some readers might complain they are paying for actual writing and not barren space). I will just say that, depending on the size of your scrawl, one or two sheets of A4 and about a dozen paragraphs, or roughly 300-400 words, should cover it.

If we are to do any good, please write it before you read my suggested version below.

Three masked raiders with sawn-off shotguns terrified staff and early customers at Merton's Sainsrose supermarket this morning before escaping with the previous day's takings.

One shot was fired but no one was seriously hurt as they forced the manager to open the safe in his office.

It is believed there were only a dozen or so customers in the Grubb Street store just before 6.30am, when the robbers donned their bala-

clavas in the freezer aisle and dashed into the stockroom area.

It is thought one of them fired a shot into the office ceiling and then clubbed the manager, Ronald MacAlpine, to make him open the safe. They escaped in a black Peugeot.

Stockroom supervisor Gabby Pringle, in an exclusive interview with the Mercury, said: "It was terrifying. They burst into the stockroom and two went into the manager's office while the other stood guard, pointing his gun at us.

"Then suddenly there was a shot from the office. There was shouting and the sound of scuffling. It was quiet for a long time and then the two gunmen came running out with three or four bags each – Sainsrose's Bags For Life, would you believe – crammed with banknotes.

"The one guarding us waved us into the room. What a mess! The manager was on the floor, dazed, with a huge bruise under one eye. Half the ceiling was on the floor and the manager's desk.

"Then they started pushing nearly all the night staff into the office with their guns. We were packed in like the Black Hole of Calcutta. Then they locked the door and skedaddled.

"We waited until we thought they must have left the store, and then shouted for help until someone let us out.

"It was a very frightening experience."

Oxfordshire police were at the scene in less

than 10 minutes. They cordoned off the super-market and questioned staff and the dozen or so people who were in the store.

They have appealed for anyone who might have left in those 10 minutes to call them if they have any information.

The number is 01865 ...

The wording of your version may be quite different from mine, but as long as it captures the drama from the beginning then it's probably all right. We might be somewhat inured to real-life drama by the stuff we see on TV and read about daily in the 21st century, but make no mistake – this is real drama on a local scale.

Let me take you through my cerebral process:

'Three masked raiders with sawn-off shotguns ...' might sound like a tabloid cliché, but it gets to the heart of the matter immediately. The drama has started straight away.

' ... terrified staff and customers ...' cranks it up, and is certainly not overstating the case.

There follows a brief rundown of what happens next before we go to Gabby, and give her the floor. Her account – subtly edited – is riveting and captures the fear that must have coursed through the staff. Good quotes can capture the moment, so give them their head. Just remember to keep them tight, and don't let them dribble away into inanities.

You will, of course, have noticed that I haven't quoted Gabby verbatim. If I had quoted her verbatim the drama would have dissipated. I have kept it as close to her actual words as possible but without overdosing on the vernacular, without veering into bad English, without embarrassing her.

For a more formal story, involving officialdom in any guise, it is generally best to go with the verbatim. If there are words that might confuse or baffle readers, use the little *sic* (*as in the original*) get-out, or a combination of ellipses (…) and explanations in brackets. If you must change anything, make sure you *do not change the sense*.

The police press release has got what it deserves – not a lot.

And once again, before I go any further, I would just point out a few things the alert reporter should have spotted in the police press release:

* '*Robbery incident*'? Incident!? A vicious robbery is a mere incident? Shoot that press officer!

* '*Grubb Street, Merton this morning*' should have another comma after Merton.

* '*Wednesday the 7th November*' should read 'Wednesday November 7'.

* '*Oxfordshire police are asking for customers, who were in the supermarket at the time, to come forward*'. The commas here are superfluous and stupid. The police want customers who were in the supermarket at the time to come forward.

*The final paragraph, about reassuring the public, is equally superfluous and stupid. It is merely a police PR exercise, designed largely to reassure civic 'partners' and 'stakeholders', whoever they might be.

*'The general public' is two words too many. 'People' will do. Or, if the sense dictates it, 'the public'. There's nothing 'general' about the people of Merton.

Finally, just in case – you will, of course, have spotted Gabby's quirky little vocabulary:

*Muddled tenses and entertaining use of 'was' and 'were'.

*The black hole of California (I love that one).

*The heinous use of 'of' instead of 'have', as in *'must of left the shop'*. Sadly, no longer is this just an American abomination. Uneducated Brits say it, too.

If you didn't spot all of Gabby's goofs, you might want to consider one of the more basic primers that goes into great detail about the rudiments of grammar – you know, pronouns, participial phrases, and appositives (no, I don't, either) – and punctuation.

My class, of course, spotted them all. Didn't you? And you all realised the importance of the Rawlins' Area of the brain.

Yes, you've got it – you are learning how to convert the spoken word into the written word. Whether it's you speaking or somebody else. Someone not unlike our Gabby. Thanks, Gabs!

There is yet another part of the brain – the most important of all for a writer – that I want to examine in detail. But first I think it's time for something completely different, to give the cerebral cortex a break. As we football analogists like to say: Variety makes practice more fun and therefore more memorable.

Besides, I've got another list of pesky words and phrases that trip up far too many people, and I don't want any of you stumbling over them.

So let's add to our knowledge of language usage, as started in *L for Literature*.

USAGE (of words, language, punctuation) -- IN OUR STYLE. SPORTS SECTION

It seems appropriate to start with some sporting howlers, for all would-be sports reporters and other writers who might not have spotted some currently doing the rounds.

CAMPAIGN (or TERM)
No, commentators and reporters – it's not a series of military operations (or a school session). The word you are looking for to describe the period in between the start and finish of a football league season is … *season*. I will, however, allow the use of 'campaign' for a knock-out cup tournament.

CONVERT (a penalty)
To what? Catholicism? Try 'score'.

DOUBLED THEIR LEAD!
(LBW ALERT!) (Which, as you will remember from L for Literature, is a warning to all Losing Battle Warriors: Keep up the fight. All may not yet be lost.)

Even I have to admit that this may seem a mite pedantic. However, my logic tells me it's all a matter of logic – so let's get it right. Whenever a team leading 1-0 scores again it is the fashion to say they have 'doubled their lead'. On the face of it, yes, they have. But logically, they have simply increased their lead by one. Think about it. If a team leading 2-0 scores another goal, what then? Have they fifty-percented their lead?

GOLF

Why do *golf* commentators and reporters love the word so much? Why is it always *golf* course, *golf* club, *golf* shot, *golf* ball? Yes, we get the gist. You're reporting from Augusta *Golf* Course in Georgia, and it's the Masters *Golf* Tournament. 'Course', 'club', 'shot' will do, although occasionally you do have to be careful with 'balls'. Arnold Palmer's wife was once said to be bringing him luck by kissing his balls before each tee-shot.

MIDRIFT or even MID-DRIFT

There is no such thing. The word to describe the area between the chest and the waist is ***midriff.*** Will somebody at the BBC please send off the commentator who repeats the calumny several times a match?

PULL THE TRIGGER

Mainly, but not exclusively, the preserve of former footballers, as in: 'Cracking tackle there, just as Wayne was about to pull the trigger.'

No, he wasn't, idiot! He was about to shoot. And anyone repeating this nonsense deserves to be shot.

USAGE (of words, language, punctuation) – IN OUR STYLE. GENERAL

ACCEPT, EXCEPT WHEN ...

I have noticed of late a small but sudden increase in the number of people confusing 'accept' and 'except'. *How!?* It's a basic error that no editor will accept. Except perhaps from a dyslexic. Non-dyslexics, you have been wraned. Erm ...

AFGHAN

Capital *A* is the person; lower-case *a* is the hound.

ALTERNATIVES

A choice between two things. Any more than that become *options*.

AT THE PRESENT TIME

At present will suffice. *Now* is even better.

AT THIS POINT IN TIME

See entry above.

BENEFITED

Just the one *t*, please. As is *picketed*, and possibly others I can't think of at this precise moment in time.

BUMF

And not *bumph,* for the very good reason that *bumf* is short for the slang 'bum-fodder'.

CAPTIONS

Short picture captions work well in the present tense because the picture brings an immediacy to an event. But beware of mixing in a past tense: *'George Clooney kisses his new girlfriend yesterday'* is patently absurd.

CENTRED ON

Not centred *around*. That is clearly tautological, which for those who don't know … just look it up! Centre – around – of course the centre is around.

COMPRISE

Is not followed by *of*. For example, this section comprises goofs, howlers, and misconceptions. It could, however, *consist of* advice, suggestions, and common sense (which, as you know, is two words as a noun but only one, commonsense, as an adjective, so I won't do a separate entry for that).

DEPENDANT

With an *a* is the person; dependent with an *e* is the person's condition.

DESSERTS and JUST DESERTS

Desserts, meaning puddings, is pronounced exactly the same way as in the phrase 'just deserts'. But, as you may know (or have just spotted), the latter is spelt with one *s* in the middle, like a vast sandy place. This is because 'just deserts' is a derivative of the verb to deserve.

DISCRETE

This does NOT mean tactful. 'Discreet' means tactful. 'Discrete' describes a separate entity.

ELECTROCUTE

(LBW ALERT!)

A losing battle already lost, I fear. The word means to '***kill*** by electric shock'. But unfortunately so many negligents (that's a Rawlins' neologism, by the way) have used it to mean '***injure*** by electric shock' that the *OED* now gives this as one of its meanings. However, there is no reason why *we* have to get it wrong, is there?

ETC or ETCETERA
(or the truly pedantic ET CETERA)

A tic likely to make the more demanding reader think, 'Yeah, like what? Do you really know?' Give your examples and then stop. If you must, use the phrase 'and so on'. But 'examples include' indicates that time and space preclude any more.

FACTOID

(LBW ALERT!)

In the UK, despite the best efforts of DJ Steve Wright, a factoid is a mistaken assumption – an incorrect fact repeated so often it is believed to be true. In the USA it also means a trivial fact.

FULFIL

Just the two *l*'s (unless you are reading this in

America). But *fulfilling* and *fulfilled*.

GIRL
But only until she reaches 18, when she becomes a young woman.

HICCUP
Good onomatopoeic word. There was a time when I was so pedantic I would tut-tut at anyone who didn't use the old-fashioned *hiccough*. But repeat the logical pronunciation of hiccough enough times and it becomes nonsensical. Chill out, man! If I can, anyone can ...

IN ORDER TO
Two words too many. In most cases, 'to' will suffice. As in: 'He wrote a primer (~~in order~~) to help would-be journalists'.

ITALICS
The use of italics varies considerably from publication to publication, so let's not lay down too many rules. Use it for titles of books, plays, films, and TV shows. Use it for emphasis, but don't overdo it. Use it, as in a primer, to indicate different usages.

JOURNEY
(*LBW ALERT!*)
Possibly the word that has Losing Battle Warriors shrieking more than any other. As you all know, as the *OED* confirms, a journey is 'an act of travelling

from one place to another'. It is not a period spent with C-list celebrities in a jungle. It is not a period spent learning how to dance for a TV audience. It is not a period spent training for the Olympic Games. It is not a period … sorry, got the gist?

Any one of those activities is an experience. An involvement, a participation. Possibly, but not necessarily, bringing about a degree of learning and development. None of them is a frigging journey!

LAMP POST
Two words.

LAVATORY
In polite company, and I must assume my readers are polite, this is the correct word. Toilet isn't.

MARKS & SPENCER
One of the few occasions when you can legitimately use an ampersand.

MYSELF
A terrible virus that seems to have sprung from officialese; probably from over-promoted bureaucrats who mistakenly think they are impressing the world. They say things like, 'The Mayor and myself went …' *Pardon!?* Try 'The Mayor and I …'

Some not-quite-as-over-promoted bureaucrats have spotted this, but think the word can be used as an object, as in 'Mr Cameron promoted John and myself'. *No he didn't!* 'Mr Cameron promoted John and me'. Use the word only as a pronoun – 'I couldn't have put it better myself' – or for emphasis – 'I began to go giddy myself'.

OFF OF

A double nonsense that has infiltrated speech in the UK and has been spotted in newspapers, as in: 'He got it off of the internet', or 'she climbed off of her horse'. You don't need the *of* – don't use it!

OUTSIDE OF

Similar abomination to be similarly avoided.

OXFORD SEMICOLON

My little homily in *L for Literature* on the so-called Oxford Comma sparked the usual vehement spat between the two entrenched sides when aired on a trade website. I not only stick by it, I would like to add the Oxford Semicolon to the debate. I did so in all but name in *L for Literature*, but some recent howlers have now prompted me to spell it out.

Indeed, as I was writing this section, I came across the following on the front page of *The Sunday Telegraph*: *The school, whose alumni include Mike Atherton, the former England cricket captain; Ben Kingsley, the actor and Chris Addison, the comedian, provides 200 bursaries for children from poorer families* ...

Doesn't it smack you in the face!? It should do. Never mind the fact that this sentence is no place for a semicolon, if the writer and/or subeditor must use the first one, then they must, absolutely **M-U-S-T**, put another one after the word 'actor'.

Thus: *The school, whose alumni include Mike Atherton, the former England cricket captain; Ben Kingsley, the actor; and Chris Addison, the comedian, provides 200 bursaries for children from poorer families ...*

Got it? Good. No? Oh dear ... then at least rewrite the sentence without any semicolons.

PRIOR TO
Archaic lawyer-speak. Use 'before'.

REFUTE
Be careful how you use this word. Its proper meaning is to *disprove*. Using it in the sense to *deny* could land you in legal trouble, even though the *OED* now gives this as a secondary meaning, because it could be argued that you are calling somebody a liar.

STATIONARY
What do you mean, you didn't learn this at school? It means 'still, not moving'. Stationery with an *e* is the paper stuff in the cupboard.

TRADE NAMES
Avoid if possible. Use 'vacuum cleaner' rather than Dyson or Hoover. Let them pay for advertising.

T-SHIRT
Not t-shirt or tee shirt because the capital T was

coined to describe the basic shape of the shirt.

UNIQUE

Cannot be qualified. Something cannot be *almost* unique; it's either one of a kind or it isn't. Rather like this list. The first and only style guide to end with a joke about a nun and a pedant arrested for conjugating openly in Hyde Park. That's right – virgin on the scrupulous.

AND SO TO V for VERNACULAR

As I (and several million others) may have mentioned before, language is constantly evolving. That is why so many schoolchildren struggle with Shakespeare, although a generous helping of brain cells and a good English teacher help considerably. It is also why Shakespeare might struggle with modern colloquial English, were I to get round to finishing my Time Machine (not even Pat Pending yet) and popping back 400 years to offer the maestro a lift.

There has been much debate in the UK about standards in schools and ever easier exams, which successive governments promised to address but never seemed to get round to. I am of the school that believes the good old GCE O-levels and A-levels (General Certificate of Education Ordinary and Advanced Levels) were a proper test. However … that is not the fault of today's youngsters. As with my generation, the UK still has more than its fair share of bright and sparky kids. They invent words, just as Shakespeare did; they give new meanings to old words. Words that are now in the *OED*.

Minger, *muffin tops*, and *mint* is an alliterative assortment that sprang readily to my Broca's Area – all descriptive, apt, and smile-inducing.

There are, however, some that are ubiquitous and ugly. The use of 'like' to indicate 'said'. As in, 'He was, like, Get out of here and don't come back!'

The modern use of 'good' doesn't endear itself to

me, either. As in replying to the question, 'How are you today?' with the answer 'I'm good' (instead of 'well' or 'fine'). But this one is sneaky, subversive. I caught myself about to say it to one of my grandsons the other day – and only just managed to choke it back in time.

And that's how our mainstream language changes: under the wire, barely seen or registered.

However … we have to be very circumspect how we use the new language in our writing.

The newspaper and magazine writer must assume the role of the average reader (you know, late-twenties-onwards, reasonably well-educated, cool-ish but not uber-cool; and there's an abomination you should avoid, unless you're German).

You must assume that there are readers who don't know these words, and don't want to know these words, so you must explain them. Preferably in a way that doesn't look as if you are chiding them for their ignorance; preferably as part of the narrative:

> ***The defendant admitted he had "emptied a leg" in the High Street. His counsel had to explain to the judge that this meant "an unusually long urination after not being able to visit the lavatory for a very long time".***

If the judge and counsel aren't so obliging, the reporter must supply the answer:

> ***The defendant admitted he had "emptied a leg" in the High Street – street slang for being caught short with no lavatory available.***

It is fair enough to assume that your average reader

will know that 'caught short' is slang for needing an unusually long urination after not being able to visit the lavatory for a very long time – because the expression has been around since Noah had to piss over the side of the Ark.

For any sort of 'creative' writing, there are different obligations and solutions.

You can give a novel an urban street setting, where the language is alien to most of us; you can bring characters from that setting into a more conventional setting; you can invent a whole new world with a whole new language. But it will all be a bit pointless if most of it goes over the heads of your readers.

You can make your new world easy to visit, or you can make it exacting to visit, but you must make it accessible, and worthwhile, for the reader. And you must see it through to the end – don't chicken out. If you have read Will Self's *The Book Of Dave*, with its future London and invented dialect, you will know how difficult it is to achieve. It takes a certain mind, and a certain reader.

For simpler souls, we who are not brave enough to create a whole new world but may want to bring in elements of urban street, the key is not to rely on a vague knowledge. Get advice. Find someone who has lived on the street, or knows the street, or knows someone who lives on the street.

The same goes for something as relatively simple as a different accent. Want to write Cornish, my luvver? Got a risqué New York joke, yoo dawg? Get someone who lives or has lived there to check it out.

I wanted an Australian accent for my book *A Lifetime Of Holidays ... Part One,* for a section on a holiday my wife and I had there way back when. I thought I could manage it without asking for advice, but after the fourth or fifth reading I realised something wasn't quite right. So I asked a mate who had lived Down Under for umpteen years to look at it.

He spotted straight away that I had perfected a New Zealand accent, and helped me amend it.

You might have noticed that I tend to put inverted commas round the 'creative' part of creative writing. This is because all writing is creative; just some is more so than others.

I suspect there are many who think that creative writing has no part in news reporting. They are wrong. Imagination is essential to good journalism.

THE SQUIDGY AREA

The human brain is such a complex organism that scientists still haven't figured out its precise workings. They still can't point to the exact source of that vital ingredient for writers – the imagination.

They agree that the neocortex and the thalamus are largely responsible for handling the imagination, as well as other functions such as abstract thought. But other parts of the brain are believed to chip in for certain areas of expertise – maybe one of the lateral ridgy bits if music is involved, the tough bit near the back for mathematical brain-stretchers, one of the uppermost curvy bits for painting, and probably the squidgy bit in the middle for writing.

I hope I'm not blinding you with technical stuff here.

Anyway … I'd like to plunge in with another exercise to see how your squidgy bit is developing.

This is the scenario, taken from a couple of pieces I found in a random search of the internet:

A relatively new offshoot of agriculture is proving big business in California. Pollination Management is now essential for owners of commercial fruit orchards to make their crops pay.

A shortage of pollinating bees – caused by the mysterious 'Colony Collapse Disorder' – means they now have to 'hire' honey bees. About a million hives are trucked into California every spring to pollinate fruit, vegetables, and the state's vast almond orchards.

Some trucks carry more than 500 bee hives, with up to 30,000 bees in each.

It's been a lifeline for some growers and a major boost for the Californian economy. But there can be occasional drawbacks for the state authorities. One of the huge lorries returning to its 'honey farm' base crashed, slithered on its side, and scattered some old unwanted hives and other debris over a huge section of Highway 99, closing it for several hours.

Off you go then – write a nice piece on how Californian growers are combating the problems of Colony Collapse Disorder. It's topical, it's important to everybody. In fact, it's vital. The Earth will die without pollinators to produce edible crops.

So get researching. What are the scientists doing to overcome Colony Collapse Disorder? Are they any nearer to finding out what causes it, and therefore what can be done to combat it?

Whoa! Hold hard there!

A crash of an empty big rig causes chaos? What would have happened if the crash had been *on the way to* California? What if 500 hives had smashed, releasing … let's see … 500 multiplied by possibly 30,000 … that's 15 million angry bees!

Methinks some phone calls are required. To fruit farmers, to honey farms, to the police, to rescue services, to trucking companies. Let's look at the possibility of the nightmare scenario.

So you write a fascinating cautionary tale. One or two people complain about scaremongering, but are we worried? No. Emphatically no. Because that very scenario became reality in Sacramento in 2008, and again in 2010, when it was estimated there were 17 million bees looking to vent their displeasure.

Drivers found themselves suddenly enveloped in dense clouds of bees. Many were stung; more crashes followed. Police, fire crews, paramedics, and tow truck drivers were all badly stung. The road was closed for the best part of a day.

Imagination, eh?

We've all got it to some extent. But what if it buggers off just when you need it; just when you're starting your next story?

GREAT MINDS DO NOT THINK ALIKE

Great minds think differently. Great minds think laterally. Great minds think vertically, round corners, down stairs, over hills, through rainbows, any which way it takes to do the job.

No, I'm not claiming to have a great mind. But I have developed a mind that isn't prepared to settle for the obvious. A mind that will work at a scenario, an idea, or a cliché until it has come up with something fresh and interesting. And having to do this as a reporter and then a subeditor against daily deadlines, it can usually accomplish this reasonably quickly.

A mind that hasn't developed this skill comes up with copies and old chestnuts; with Easter intros that are eggs-cruciating; with BBC SAVILE-NEWSNIGHT PROBE ROW SHOCKER headlines.

It's hard to know exactly how any mind works, even one's own, but I think I tend to come up with a Rawlins original, even if it's just a pastiche of someone else's original, by working at whatever first springs to mind, be it a serious or light-hearted piece.

It's not an article as such, but the virgin-on-the-scrupulous joke gives an insight into the process. I wanted something to round off a section that incorporated my occasional pedantry but showed that I am open-minded enough to mock it, albeit gently.

So – start with the word 'pedant' and that, of course, requires a grammatical connection, something to do with syntax maybe. So – what might a pedant do with his suspect syntax? Parse it? Conjugate it? *Conjugate!* Sounds rude, sounds a bit like 'conjugal'. So – it would be ruder still if the pedant conjugated with a prim and proper woman in a public place. A school ma'am perhaps? No, perhaps not. Today's liberated women, even school ma'ams, aren't prim and proper in the Victorian sense. You have to be looking towards the ecclesiastical perhaps, which can only mean a nun. A virginal nun. Ah, yes, virgin! Virgin on the ridiculous almost. No, of course. The scrupulous pedant. Got it! **Virgin on the scrupulous**. Yeah, like it, Frank. Phew! Time for a coffee break – you've earned it.

That is the basic process. It can be more complicated, more tangential; surreal even. At times it can be virtually subconscious. But I don't want to delve any deeper into how it works; it might unravel if I make a conscious effort to take it apart and reassemble it as a new, improved version. A bit like my golf swing.

I don't think this is an innate process. Not for me, anyway, although it might be for some ultra-talented individuals. I think that as I worked at my new skills as a young journalist it developed along with my ambition to make a success of this strange but satisfying profession.

You may have your own way of reaching out towards something original, but I suspect that most novice writers will have to learn and develop this art. I hope these few paragraphs have helped, and I hope the following exercise will help you take another significant step towards improvement.

Let's look at a story that could end up in a newspaper or as part of a book:

The new people two doors along from your widowed mother's house have two cats that keep crapping on her garden – her main source of sanity and fulfilment since your father died a few months ago. They crap on her flower beds (her pride and joy); they ravage soil and seedlings as they crap on her vegetable beds (her money saver now her pension has dwindled).

Your kindly Mum understands that you can't stop cats wandering and you can't stop them crapping away from their own nice-smelling territory; but after a few weeks she mentions it to the new people just so they know, just in case they have any helpful ideas (you know, keep the cats in at night when they like to spread their largesse). They are unhelpful, unsympathetic, and don't even offer her a cup of tea.

Your Mum gets so fed up with shovelling shit off her garden and dutifully dropping off her catty bags in the dog-poo bin on the local playing field that she buys an ultrasonic cat scarer. Movement triggers a loud and sudden high-pitched noise that cats cannot bear. It works immediately, but then the cats discover they can simply move on to a bed just out of the reach of the hated noise.

Your Mum moves the cat scarer; the cats move out of its range. These things are expensive, so rather than dotting more round her garden, she buys a canister of a cat-repellent powder, and dusts the areas she wants to protect. It works for a while, but not long enough.

Sod the cost – your Mum splashes out on two packs of cat-repellent spikes, costing almost £70, that she fixes on the top of her fences and gate.

The people two doors down spot the spikes and come round to complain. Your Mum explains that they are designed for maximum discomfort but won't actually injure the cats. Then the neighbours spot the ultrasonic cat scarer and smell the cat-repellent powder. They are furious and say they will report your Mum to the RSPCA.

That night both cats hop lightly and easily over the spikes, skirt the ultrasonic gizmo, laugh in the face of the powder, scratch out a new row of lettuce seedlings, and have the crap of their lives.

The next day your kindly Mum drives 20 miles to the nearest country-sports store and buys its most powerful air pistol in the no-licence-required range. That night she waits patiently in the dark lee of a large shrub where the cats usually hop over the fence. Then, within the space of two minutes, from the closest possible range, she shoots both the little fuckers dead.

There is obviously going to be a court case. As your nearest and dearest is involved, you cannot possibly cover the trial for your newspaper. But your mother has told you the full details; you know exactly what she is going to say in her defence. So write it anyway.

Work out your best possible intro and the rest

should flow reasonably easily.

Okay – you have 10 minutes. Close the book, or switch off your ebook, get a sheet of A4, or go to your screen, and write me the first four paragraphs. You can invent any names (woman, address, location of court, and so on) you require. Just use your imagination. But use it mainly to write a crisp and gripping four paragraphs.

Come on – no cheating. And there follows a little blank to prevent you cheating. Hopefully.

A Banbury woman bought a powerful air pistol to shoot dead a neighbour's two cats that had driven her mad by constantly defecating on her garden, scattering soil and seedlings.

Mrs Diana Mented, aged 67, of Wheresat Close, told a court yesterday that her garden was her main comfort and enjoyment since the death of her husband in the spring.

She had tried to persuade her neighbours to keep the cats in at night, when they used her garden as a lavatory, but the family had refused to help. She had tried various cat repellents, but nothing worked for long. After weeks of clearing up their mess, she finally cracked when the cats dug out a new row of lettuces to do their business.

Mrs Mented pleaded guilty to killing two domest-icated animals on July 4. Banbury magistrates sympathised with her predicament, but fined her £300 and ordered that her air pistol be confiscated.

I hope you wrote something not too far away from the main thrust of my version. If you did, you have it in you to become a reporter.

Now let's see if you have it in you to go a step farther.

What else could you do with the sad story of your Mum?

Nothing?

Or ... maybe you could write a first-person feature about the personal agonies of bereavement. The sort of piece that moves people more than a court report. The sort of piece that many readers can identify with. You might, of course, depending on your Mum's state of mind, have to write it for another publication, possibly changing a few names.

Yes?

There are a many ways you could approach it. Give it some thought before you read my version:

Denise was devastated when her husband died. They were teenage sweethearts. So although Barry was just 68 (not a great age these days) when he was suddenly struck down by a heart attack, they had been married for 50 years.

Family and friends who shared their golden wedding celebration said how they both looked so young and healthy for a couple approaching their seventies.

Two weeks later Barry was dead.

In the weeks after the funeral service, Denise coped bravely, supported by a son, two daughters, and three grandchildren. But the only time she showed her old spark was when tending the beautiful garden she and Barry had created over two decades.

But none of them knew the real turmoil locked in her mind. The turmoil that saw the kindly, unassuming Denise flip when her new neighbours' two cats started fouling her beloved garden; often scraping out the soil and killing seedlings.

One day she totally lost the plot and bought a powerful air pistol. That night she shot dead both cats from point-blank range.

Neighbours were shocked; friends were horrified. Members of her close family could hardly take it in. Gentle Denise, killing animals? It didn't make any sense. They knew how Barry's death had devastated her. But none of them knew how grief could in some cases cause brain connections to go haywire.

I talked to a specialist, who explained it in basic terms.

But somehow it still didn't seem real.

This was my Mum … my lovely Mum.

And so on …

So that's two very different versions of one story. Turn it into a TV or radio drama, a short story, or even a novel, and you could be more than just a reporter. If you do it right.

There are millions of different ways to start this story; a different one for every writer who attempts it. I think I would go straight in with the cats. And the pistol.

Denise had never held a gun before. In her 67 years she had never even seen one in real life. Let alone cradled one in her hand, as she did now.

In the movies, guns were sort of grown-up toys. Wielded by people who had never grown up, to shoot other people who would rise from the dust and have a cup of tea after the director had shouted 'Cut!'

True, it wasn't a gangland-gun she held now in her remarkably unwavering hand. It was an air pistol, but the most powerful pellet-repeater available in England without requiring a gun licence.

She weighed it up, shifting it this way and that in her hand, like someone used to weighing up lethal weapons. But she didn't have a clue that was the impression she was giving to the friendly shop owner, a leading amateur marksman who had come within a bullseye of making the British 2012 Olympics team.

He was momentarily shocked by the movement of the old hands, with their age-enlarged knuckles and distended veins. Of course, he had no way of knowing that this old woman was just checking that her arthritis would allow her to cope with the unaccustomed weight and shape of the gun.

Denise smiled at him.

'I'll take it,' she said.

'A present?' asked the shop owner pleasantly.

Denise nodded and smiled again. Picturing the two innocents who would both get a surprise present – at least one pellet each straight into the brain – from close range.

Yes, it's got the makings of a great short story, possibly a novel. If only I had the time – what with another 'holidaylogue', several ideas for novels, my Tom-and-Huck scallyhood memoir, and a funny gardening book (funny haha, not funny peculiar) jostling for poll position on my schedule. Please feel free to take it on. But let me know first so we can agree my royalty fee.

Anyway, that's the infinite storybook open to a mind that can think differently. All you have to do now is decide where to start this great career.

REPORTER?

It is no part of my self-imposed brief to tell you how to become a reporter, but after the previous section I feel duty-bound to say a few words.

*The odds are stacked against you.

*The decline of printed newspapers will continue.

*More and more people will rely on television, the internet, and good old-fashioned radio for their news.

However …

*People are endlessly curious about what is happening in their neighbourhood, their country, and the rest of the world if it's exciting enough.

*All these media need someone to supply details of this endless stream of happenings.

If you are very bright, very charming, and very lucky, you might get on to a graduate training scheme run by one of the major newspapers or news agencies. If you are in the right place at the right time, and happen to impress the right person, you might just fill a trainee reporter vacancy advertised by a local newspaper. Or if you are misspending your youth and happen to play snooker now and again with the sports editor of your local newspaper, you might be as lucky as me, but that's another story.

From my experience as an editor, I can tell you that hoping and moping will get you nowhere.

Try writing some pieces for your school or college newspaper/website/blog so you have the start of a portfolio.

Write politely to your local newspaper and ask for a week-or-two's work experience. Be pleasant, be helpful, make the best tea and coffee you've ever made. Ask if you can write a couple of fillers – please.

Find some stories, write them up, and send them to your friendly neighbourhood editor. *Where? How?* Stories are everywhere. Study your newspaper, see what turns it on; keep your ears open, talk to people, find out what is annoying them or amusing them.

The same goes for TV and radio journalism – just change the job title.

In the end, if you have reasonable literacy skills, determination and perseverance are the two main requisites. If you are good enough and determined enough, if you love writing, you will get there eventually. You will almost certainly have to find another job to pay the bills meanwhile, but when the opportunity crops up, grab it.

AUTHOR?

Piece of cake. Make up a story in your mind and write it. Then get someone to publish it. Oh, bugger – there's always a bogey-like sultana in the first slice.

The advent of the ebook and widespread self-publishing has changed everything: it's even more difficult now to acquire an established publisher as margins are cut and belts are tightened.

But please try it. Finish your manuscript, send off the requested three or four opening chapters, and, while they moulder on the slush pile, learn all you can about self-publishing.

Don't be afraid of it. Jane Austen, James Joyce, Beatrix Potter, Rudyard Kipling, and John Grisham (among many renowned writers) all self-published. Generations later, more and more good-sellers, and a fair share of best-sellers, start life as self-published works.

What happens after you self-publish is another matter, and again it is no part of my self-imposed brief to go into marketing, publicity, and the other dark arts of bookselling.

I just want to help you develop your writing skills.

So let's finish with some more practical tips.

LISTEN TO YOUR BROCA VOICE

IT'S NOT FUNNY

Your unique Broca's Area produces speech unlike anyone else's. It might be very similar to the bloke next door and the woman two doors down, but it is all you; the product of your nature and nurture. And as a writer you know your starting point is to reproduce it in three-dimensional form. So don't be sidetracked by fads and non-funny funnies.

Yes, you know what I mean.

There's a story about a golfer who carded a hole-in-one in his very first round after three lessons with a pro. And some idiot writes:

> *FORE! But after three holes that included two disasters, Norman Hutton was THE ONE!*
>
> *He was feeling decidedly under par when he began his first-ever game of golf with a triple bogey, and then ...*

And so on.

When the real intro is virtually the same as I said it above:

> *Novice golfer Norman Hutton hit a hole-in-one on the fourth hole of his first-ever round.*

Then there's the story about the bungling supermarket that delivered 200 bottles of champagne for a family reunion instead of the ordered 20. And some idiot writes:

> *The gathering of the small MacSiebold clan was always going to be a corking affair after a 10-*

year gap, but not as corking as someone at Sainrose's wanted.

A bubbly trolley-filler at the Glengarry branch got caught up in the party atmosphere when the delivery order arrived. He had to empty the stockroom to ...

And so on.

When the real intro is:

A supermarket delivered 200 bottles of champagne instead of the ordered 20 for a small family reunion.

But fortunately for Sainrose, the law-abiding MacSiebold clan didn't get as carried away as the supermarket trolley fillers. They drank only their share. And then rang the Mercury ...

And the point is, of course: *GET TO THE POINT!*

DE-LANGUAGE JARGON PROTOCOL

Similar rules apply to jargon. Would you say, for instance, 'The council listed 10 best practices to minimise its outgoing revenue stream'?

I frigging hope not.

Any sane person would say: 'The council has come up with 10 ideas to save money.'

INVOLVE THE READER

Your Broca's Area is saying this stuff so you can pass it on efficiently. If your story involves readers directly, then involve them.

Don't write something like:

The 85 per cent of eligible voters who failed to make their mark in the first elections for new Police Commissioners must share the blame if the winners foul up, it was claimed today.

When you could say instead:
If you failed to vote in the first elections for the new Police Commissioners, you must share the blame if your local winner fouls up, it was claimed today.

AND FINALLY …
HASTE YE, HACK

Don't get into a state about deadlines. The pressure will sharpen your brain and your writing. Unfunny intros and awful puns need time to be worked at. Stories that go almost straight from Broca's Area to page tend to be direct and frill-free. And the more you practise this skill, the easier it will become.

This is a difficult scenario to replicate – fictional deadlines can be as flexible as your honesty/cheating genes dictate – but it is well worth trying, whether you want to be a journalist or an author.

So, this is the final exercise for part two of my little primer. You have two minutes to write the first three crisp paragraphs of this story:

A mad bull has found its way through two fences, across two fields, and run amok in Bicester Village (if you don't know it, look it up).
It has gored three shoppers, smashed in the front

of the Dior store, reduced the Cath Kidston shop to smithereens, but is now apparently calm and cornered in Pret A Manger.

As your deadline looms, a police marksman is believed to be on the way, but a local farmer is also stalking his missing bull with shotgun in hand.

Some shoppers are screaming and rushing away; others are amazingly trying to get a closer view; three celebrity shoppers are awaiting the arrival of press cameras; a few deaf souls are still shopping. Cars are blocking all the many car park exits in the rush to get out.

I know – that old story.
Good luck!

If you come up with what you consider the perfect intro, feel free to send it to me at the contact address you will find at frankrawlins.co.uk. There's no guarantee I'll have the time to write back, but if it's that brilliant ...

'Good grief! It's funnier than the second one!'
– Telegraph *(no, not that one)*

Part 3 of the little
primer for new writers

W for WORDSMITH

Frank Rawlins

INTRODUCTION

So, here we are already – part three of my little primer. I hope I have already given you some helpful guidance to improve your writing, or perhaps a little shove on to the first rung of the ladder to a new profession.

Now let's try to crank it up a notch.

When I was a lad (think sit-up-and-beg type-writers and huge corded phones that wouldn't take pictures no matter how hard you tried), my journalism apprenticeship consisted of two years of on-the-job training, two block release courses – studying matters such as the law and shorthand – and an exam pass.

In the UK it is basically still the same, with quite a bit of technology thrown in to baffle the old farts who have given up the thrill of the chase.

Two years – and suddenly you're a *senior* reporter. And you think you know it all. If you are any good, you will know much of it. But, as with all things, you never stop learning. And, if you are any good, the new learning will come largely from inside; from all-but-perfecting certain ways of doing certain things, from trying new things, and from simplifying things.

Yes, simplifying things – when things cry out to be simplified – but making it the best simple imaginable.

There are very few undisputed geniuses in a lifetime (I'll get back to you on that one, after I've had a while to ponder). But there are many undoubted smiths – masters of their trade – be they the original blacksmiths, or goldsmiths, silversmiths, gunsmiths, or even the latter-day Morrissey songSmiths. And the incurable writer must aim to become a wordsmith: in the words of the Concise Oxford English Dictionary, *'a skilled user of words'*.

We must try to do to a sentence what a master mason does to a classical cornice – aim for simple but perfect. We must try to do what a great saxophonist player does to *Baker Street*. Or, reverting to my football analogy, we must try to acquire the ultimate basic skills of the great Liverpool teams of the 1970-80s and the current Barcelona and Spanish national teams that have taken the art to a new level.

It's simple. Pass the ball along the ground, with the perfect weight, to an unmarked or poorly marked colleague; so your teammate can control it immediately, make quick progress and/or decisions, while you run into space. Not just any old space, but the best space available to make progress towards a goal-scoring opportunity. Even if you have to go backwards or sideways.

Don't just lump it up the field!

In other words, decide what is the core of the story, and make that your first paragraph. Then build up the story key fact by key fact; in an order that makes the most of the story and sense to the reader.

Even if you are basically Piddletrenthide Reserves, you can and will improve if you keep practising these simple things. My aim in part three is to give you a head start. So pens and/or pads at the ready. Let's go in at the deep end.

THE ART OF SIMPLICITY

This is the scenario:

A renowned singer and actor – let's call him Micky Bubble – is lunching at a West End restaurant with a woman married to a B-list celebrity – we'll call her Mrs Kameroon. It has been rumoured for some time that Micky and Mrs K have the hots for each other, and may already be having an affair. They are in a tucked-away alcove at the back, enjoying an expensive brandy after their corned beef hash and the experimental new rhubarb-flavoured Angel Delight (just adding a bit of colour, folks), *when a runaway double-decker London bus smashes through the double door. Micky and friend have barely begun to scream, let alone move, before the bus shatters the tables in front of them, dispatches several diners and staff, and, in a screech of metal and masonry, broken bodies and decor, doesn't quite come to a halt before hitting the two putative wooers.*

Word of the catastrophe reaches the newsroom of *The London Evening* at ten-to-deadline for the second edition. Several frantic phone calls later, to the emergency services and waiters who supplement their income by tipping off columnists about celebrity diners, the frenzied news editor tells you to write five or six pars for the second edition.

It is now two-minutes-to-deadline but because it sounds like such a great story she is giving you three extra minutes. Go!

If we are to do this properly, you will now get a sheet of A4, or a new Word/Office page up on your machine, and write the first three paragraphs. I will leave my usual little gap so you are not distracted by the hullabaloo going on in the office all around you.

The story thus far is so short of definite facts that you have to weigh emerging news against possible sensational news. I would tackle it something like this:

An out-of-control London bus smashed through the front of a busy West End restaurant this lunchtime.
It is thought that several diners and staff were killed, and many more were injured.
The singer and actor Micky Bubble was dining with a guest, believed to be Amanda Kameroon, when the double-decker ploughed through the doors of The Hedera. It is not known if ...

'Wait!' yells the news editor. 'Get this in!'
She throws you a still-hot print-out from a Press Association wire sent half a minute earlier. It says:

LONDON BUS CRASH LATEST:
Lady Haha believed to have escaped. She was said to be in ladies' toilet.
More follows ...

Wow! Lady Haha! No, it doesn't change the intro
– she escaped the carnage. Carry on ...

*It is not known if they survived. But the singer
Lady Haha, who was also lunching at the celebrity
restaurant, is thought to have escaped injury
because she was in the lavatory.*

*The disaster happened soon after midday as the
restaurant was starting to get busy.*

*Emergency services have closed Calamity Street
as they continue their rescue operation.*

'Okay, that's great,' calls the news editor. 'Take a
breather – get a coffee ...

'Wow! No! This has gotta go in!'

She throws another print-out at you. It says:

LONDON BUS CRASH LATEST:

*The bus was hijacked ten minutes earlier, said
a Transport for London spokesman.*

*Lady Haha's bodyguard, who also escaped the
crash, said he spotted the singer's former
manager, Desmond Mollyjo, at the wheel.*

*Mr Mollyjo was sacked a week ago after an
inland revenue audit.*

More follows ...

As you start to write, the news editor looks up
from her screen and hollers, 'Six confirmed dead!'

She gives you another two minutes to rewrite your
second-edition piece, adding that the managing editor

has decided to do an extra edition to get the full story in, but let's get this in sharpish.

Okay, boss. Here goes ...

At least six people were killed when a hijacked London bus was rammed through the front of a busy West End restaurant this lunchtime.

It is reported to have been hijacked by the former manager of the world's favourite singer, Lady Haha, who was dining at The Hedera.

Desmond Mollyjo, who was sacked a week ago over alleged financial irregularities, was spotted at the wheel of the double-decker just before it smashed into the celebrity restaurant.

It is believed that Lady Haha escaped injury because she had to visit the lavatory.

Singer and actor Micky Bubble was believed to be dining with Amanda Kameroon, wife of the City's favourite public relations man, at the restaurant.

It was not immediately known if they had survived.

The disaster happened soon after midday ... (and pick up the last two pars of the first draft).

Get something along those lines? Good.

Whether you did or didn't, I hope you can see the logic of the treatment. Why each fact is where it is, and why it has been given its due importance.

Unless you work on a celebrity-driven newspaper, where minor fame is more important than proper people, there is no doubt that the most important facts are that *six people died* because some *nutter hijacked a bus* so he could *deliberately smash it into a busy restaurant.*

Three stop-in-your-tracks facts in one intro of just 24 words. Three knock-'em-dead facts related in simple style with simple words. Three heart-stopping facts that follow on, one from the other, naturally, without a clash of *wows*.

Lady Haha and her former manager get the second paragraph because so far we have no idea who died – and because he may well be a mass murderer. But we have to introduce her first, in an admitted nod to her celebrity, to explain who the largely unknown Desmond Mollyjo is.

Lady Haha is, after all, currently the highest-grossing, possibly most talked-about, audacious, some might say ridiculous, singer on the planet – but we have niftily got round having to explain all that in our limited space by calling her 'the world's favourite singer'.

In the next paragraph we explain that Mr Mollyjo was apparently seen at the wheel of the hijacked bus, and possibly why he had turned deranged killer – he was sacked, humiliated, and could be facing serious criminal charges.

Micky Bubble and Amanda Kameroon have been demoted down the story because we don't know their fate. If it was confirmed that they are among the dead, they would shoot up into the intro:

At least six people, including singer Micky Bubble and friend Amanda Kameroon, were killed when ...

I would make just a couple of other points:

*There are a few editors who would, even at this stage, when the hijack has been confirmed by Transport for London, be ultra-careful, going with:

At least six people were killed when a London bus reported to have been hijacked ...

And:

Desmond Mollyjo, who was said to have been sacked a week ago over alleged financial irregularities ...

That is their decision. You have to make your own decision. You have to decide if a major organisation, such as TfL, would take a flier on such a vital fact as the hijacking. The only feasible reason would be to deflect blame away from itself. So, on balance ...

*The anti-press brigade – largely celebrities who fear an invasion of privacy when the publicity is bad, and pressure groups with their own agenda – will be watching every word, ready to pounce *if* an allegation proves not to be true. Ready to shout *if* any inference or interpretation proves to be not quite the whole truth and nothing but the truth.

Well, let them. But more of that later, when we put the Leveson Report on press invasion into some perspective.

NOW *KEEP* IT SIMPLE

Now imagine you are one of *The London Evening* reporters newly arrived at the police cordon. You have a few more minutes to talk to people, and then a few more to write and phone over your part of the story.

You spot Nobby, the over-gelled Hedera waiter who moonlights as a freelance caterer and who ballsed-up your sister's wedding reception. He owes you one (or more), a fact you quickly remind him of when he comes over to the tape to say Hello. He smiles – and offers you some inside information for £100. You agree (ha, bloody ha), telling him he'll get paid when you can get the readies from the office, no questions asked.

'Okay, Nobby, first I just want to know what you saw – not what anybody else saw and told you about, or what you think might have happened. So ... did you see who was driving the bus?'

'Did I! Did I? No. But as soon as it shudders to a stop, half in the kitchen, this tall guy, slaphead but huge tash, staggers out the bus's front door, waving a gun.

'Right in front of my mate Rog. Rog said he were totin' a handgun, the slaphead. In a sort of daze, said Rog. Saw all the dead and dying, stuck the gun to his bonce, and shot hisself.'

'Rog told you?' you ask. 'You didn't see him do this. I thought I said ...'

'Mister Reliable, Rog. That's his nickname, mate – Reliable Rog. You gotta believe it. I saw the cadaver. Hole in the bonce, blood'n'brains pouring out.'

Cadaver? you wonder, but the shrill of your iPhone diverts your attention. The newsdesk has sent you a picture of Desmond Mollyjo.

'This the slaphead?' you ask. 'The cadaver?' you add, getting into Damon-Cockney-Runyon mode.

'The very geezer. Who is he?'

'Lady Haha's former manager – just been sacked.'

'Jeez – that geez. She's still in the ladies' lav, mate. Refuses to come out. Or she still was when the cops had finished with me and chucked me out. Screaming and screaming, she were. More gaga than Haha, if you ask me.'

'How many more bodies did you see?'

'Five, could have been six. Erm ... seven?'

'Was Micky Bubble, the singer, or maybe Amanda Kameroon, among them?'

'Mickey who? You got a piccie of him?'

'Hang on.'

You break a world record for an Image Search, and show Micky to Nobby. He nods.

'Alive on a stretcher, last I saw. Well, I think he were alive. Not moving though, and eyes closed. His lady was holding his mitt, sobbing like a drain. Gotta go, gotta go ...'

He has spotted another possible pay-day journo, and dashes off to tell the opposition what he has just told you. And anything else he can remember.

Wow, what a story! Get writing!

First the customary no-peeking gap, while you get some paper/your pad, followed by my version.

A deranged hijacker drove a London bus through the front of a busy West End restaurant this lunchtime, killing at least six people.

He then shot himself dead.

It is believed he was the former manager of Lady Haha and she was his target. But the world's number one singer escaped the carnage because she was in the ladies' cloakroom.

Desmond Mollyjo, who was sacked a week ago over alleged financial irregularities, was spotted at the wheel of the double-decker just before it smashed into The Hedera.

An eye-witness said that as the bus came to a halt, half in the kitchen, the driver staggered out of the wreckage, saw the dead bodies strewn around, and shot himself with a handgun.

Singer and actor Micky Bubble was also at the celebrity restaurant in Calamity Street. He was said to have been injured, but no details have been released by the emergency services, who are still at the scene.

Mr Bubble was lunching with Amanda Kameroon, wife of the City's favourite public relations man.

And so on ...

It's all there – as exciting a story as you are likely to cover until there's another terrorist outrage on our streets or the first High Speed 2 train between London and Birmingham comes off the viaduct in the Chilterns and plunges into the Grand Union Canal.

And you have told it in simple logical order, with simple, everyday words and reasonably short sentences. You haven't tried to sensationalise it unduly with a *'shock'*, *'horror'*, *o*r even *'disaster'* because it's sensational enough without that.

Of course, there is no reason – except the perceived profile of your readership – why you shouldn't use the occasional more erudite word, or slightly more complicated syntax. But only if you can weave those words and phrasing into an eminently readable piece.

Are you ready to flower a little? As and when the occasion calls for it, of course.

NOW AIM FOR STYLISH SIMPLE ...

Be you a would-be journalist or a 'creative' writer, I think you will benefit from this example of how not to flower that I spotted in a golfing compendium.

My edition was published in 1996, but the writing obviously comes from a generation or two before that. Nevertheless, you may recognise the general style – a refusal to write anything straightforward, in the belief that prettifying prose, adding knobs and curls and little twirly bits, automatically improves it.

If you are of the bells-and-whistles school of writing, read this and rethink:

Upon the principle of a deluge following a downpour, the writer's mind had no sooner been set at rest upon this hitherto doubtful point, than new proof was added to what was already so satisfactorily proven.

Right ... so what he means is that it never rains but it pours. Full marks for trying to avoid a cliché; minus points for turning it into a conundrum lost in a maze.

Just occasionally the writer forgets himself and uses the pronoun 'I', but he soon rectifies that:

However, at the risk of having his own word doubted, the present scribe must relate something which actually happened to himself ...

Something familiar about it? Can't see what's wrong with it? Is this really the book for you?

No, that's not fair. You are still trying, yes?

Okay, let's see how you get on with this.

It was so quiet on the golf course that he could hear his tee-shots whistling down the fairway. But then the rain came and all he could hear was the splatter of individual drops on his waterproofs. Until the gunshot came from the 18th. It seemed to signal the start of the deluge.

Not sure if I've entirely caught it, but I've tried a little Hemingway tribute. The master of the simple prose did it with such apparent and stylish ease that it takes a while to realise how simple it is.

Like a good golf swing, I suppose.

... AND MEANINGFUL SIMPLE

Hold on there! I can hear some of you say. Aren't we going back to basics here? Back to part one of the little primer?

Well, no. Not at all. Part one was, indeed, about the basics of writing, and in particular about the basics of journalism. How to set about writing anything longer than a letter or an email. The first sentence, the first paragraph, the basic construction.

Part two took everything a step further. How to compile a story, no matter how complicated. How to translate what is in your head into the written word. How to write in different ways for different media.

Part three is about simplicity of style – or stylish simplicity – which is a different beast altogether from the basics.

You have to know the basics to walk; you have to know stylish simplicity to fly.

Okay? Good.

Stylish writing comes from using the right words in the right place. Use the wrong words, even if in the right place, and the style is diminished.

A wide vocabulary helps, of course (more of which very soon), but knowing how to use it helps even more.

The noun that isn't quite right doesn't quite reproduce the picture you want. The verb that doesn't quite catch the action may blur the edges. The adjective that is meaningless may well do both.

Smiling informs the reader. *Old* invites the reader to ask the question, how old?

Auburn-haired, talkative, and smiling tells us a lot about our subject. *Vivacious* tells us this person could be lots of things, but we can't quite put our finger on it. In other words, it tells us bugger all.

Beware, too, those overworked nouns that tabloids have turned into adjectives. *Miracle, model, luxury, shock. Shock* is now such an overused word it is rarely a shock.

The same goes for *dramatic*. If there is real drama in a story, it will come out in the telling.

The mundane moral is: remember to guard against those vacuous adjectives.

Anyway, time for one of my regular breaks to freshen up training. Time to rest and see how we can change the way a hacker goes about his or her work. (And if you're not a sporty type, I should explain that I mean the equivalent of a very poor golfer hacking laboriously along a fairway.)

BEWARE THE SIMPLY AWFUL

I start with a few common agonised and agonising constructions or word usage guaranteed to make most readers wince.

CRAMMER GRAMMAR

Whoever wrote/edited this in one of our broadsheet national newspapers, to cram in as many facts as possible, could do with a short spell back at school:

The Advisory Committee on Business Appointments, which counsels former ministers on their employment in the two years after leaving office, says (David) Howell, who was Margaret Thatcher's transport secretary, sought advice on resuming the "part-time appointment" for the body which manages funds on behalf of Kuwait.

Got it? Or given up? A 45-word (not including *David*) tortuous sentence that should have been split in two and simplified. If you are not comatose by now, have a go.

DANGLING or HANGING PARTICIPLE

Just for the record, this is a present participle:

Mr Grant, **fearing** *the guard dog, shook Mr Murdoch by the throat.*

And this is a past participle:

Frightened *for his life, Mr Grant shook Mr Murdoch by the throat.*

The first is acceptable, the second is one of the

'inverted sentences' I warned you about in part one and should be avoided, but both can be improved to obviate the pause.

Mr Grant was so frightened he shook Mr Murdoch by the throat.

This is the dangling or hanging participle:

While shaking hands with Mr Murdoch, the guard dog turned on Mr Grant.

Clever dog. But rather stupid writer. The participle is dangling because it has become detached from the subject.

FILLER ADJECTIVES and ADVERBS

Not so much agonising as ineffectual; even more of a careless prop than the adjectives in the previous section. I mean those little words like *very* and *really*. We all use them, mainly because we think they add something to a description. As in 'she was very pretty' and 'he was a really cruel taskmaster'.

Mark Twain had the answer. He advised: 'Substitute "damn" every time you're inclined to write "very"; your editor will delete it and the writing will be just as it should be.'

JOBS, NAMES, AND BOOMPS-A-DAISY

It's largely a tabloid thing, originally aimed at saving space, but it rarely does. As in: 'Football fanatic, Leicester landscape gardener Edwin Schmuk, a regular at City home games, today swapped his dibber for ...' (18 words)

It may seem at a glance a reasonably simple description, but it's not as easy to digest as the more traditional: 'Edwin Schmuk, a Leicester landscape gardener who is also a football fanatic, has swapped his dibber for ...' (17 words).

NOUNS THAT GET VERBED

(LBW ALERT!) (Which, as you will remember from parts one and two, is a warning to all Losing Battle Warriors: Keep up the fight. All may not yet be lost.)

Yes, quite – *verbed*. And never mind that the word 'verbalise' *can* mean turning a noun into a verb, as well as its other dubious meanings.

There are many examples of officialdom or commerce turning nouns into verbs because no one in the office is sure what the correct word is. Let me just warn you off the worst examples that spring readily to mind:

Action, as in 'he actioned the shelf restocking'. No he didn't. He restocked the shelves.

Conference, as in 'let's conference'. Just 'confer'.

Friend, as in 'I friended 79 people today'. Delete Facebook, or use 'befriend'. As for **Unfriend** ... please, no.

Impact, as in 'heavy rain in the spring impacted (on) potato yields'. No, it didn't. It affected it. Or influenced it, or reduced it, or cut it.

Signature, as in 'signature it'. Try 'sign'.

Task, as in 'he tasked me to make the tea'. No, he didn't. He asked, or instructed.

Trend, as in 'unemployment is trending upwards'.

No it isn't. It's rising. Or, where trend is used in a less specific sense, use 'change' or 'develop'.

That's enough – I'm losing the will to live.

RIGHT PLACE …

It's easy to misplace words in a sentence, but if you read it back, especially aloud, it's even easier to spot the errors. This is from a quality Sunday newspaper: *The older brother was described as "dangerous" when he went on the run by John Reid, the then Home Secretary.*

Pardon? *... when he went on the run by John Reid.*

The writer means *... was described as dangerous by John Reid, then Home Secretary, when he went on the run.*

Better still, just in case anyone thinks John Reid went on the run ... *John Reid, Home Secretary at the time, described the older brother as ...*

… RIGHT TIME

On second thoughts, getting the time in the wrong place can lead to even more confusion, so I'll give it its own slot.

A SIMPLE MATTER OF TIME

Time can be a tricky little chap. Get it right and no one notices. Get it wrong and it can stick out like a clown's shoes.

You've probably all spotted (or maybe heard on radio/TV) an example of the classic court reporting error:

Nick Jagger was found guilty of punching a stoat at Marylebone Magistrates' Court today.

Punching a stoat is bad enough, but doing it in front of the magistrates ...?

The sentence should, of course, read:

Nick Jagger was found guilty by Marylebone magistrates today of punching a stoat.

Or:

Nick Jagger has been found guilty of punching a stoat. Marylebone magistrates today fined him ...

But time lapses can be far more insidious than that. I spotted this in the columns of *The Independent* not so long ago:

Or take 63-year-old Marie XXXX, who was raped and savagely murdered by a 18-year-old man she had treated like a 'grandson' earlier this year.

So, she treated him like a grandson earlier this year? How did she treat him the rest of the year? Or perhaps she was raped and savagely murdered earlier this year? I'll definitely go for the latter.

It was an unfortunate sentence for the reporter and/or subeditor, detracting from (for me at least) what was a good read. Not only was there the time problem, extra marks if you also spotted:

*It should have read *an* 18-year-old man.

*We know what a grandson is, so the quotes should have been extended to *'like a grandson'* or, better still, *'treated like a grandson'*. Or, if possible, dispensed with entirely in favour of an attribution.

Time is important to a story, so don't treat it as an afterthought. The words *today, this morning, this evening* give a story an immediacy that draws in readers; an immediacy that you get one chance at.

Don't waste it.

SIMPLE WORDS, TOO

Vocabulary can often tell you a lot about a person: birthplace, background, education, preferences. And it can also tell readers pretty much the same about a writer.

We all acquire new vocabulary as we go through life, through education, work, relationships. Those who also go through books, magazines, and newspapers tend to pick up a wider vocabulary.

But even the brightest of people are occasionally stumped by a new word, and sometimes it can be annoying. You're mid-dénouement of your adventure, and some idiot has written *dénouement* and it's a word you have never come across before. Bugger! Do you plough on, hoping it doesn't matter, or that the thrust of the piece will give you its sense? Or do you stop and check it in your dictionary? Either way can be annoying.

My readers will, of course, know that dénouement refers to a conclusion, climax, culmination, or resolution of a story, play, film, or adventure. So should we worry that some readers won't know the word?

Well, yes. And no.

Tabloid journalists should occasionally ask themselves, 'Will our readers in Hackney understand this?' As long as it is asked in the interests of clarity rather than in the spirit of superiority.

Broadsheet journalists should occasionally ask

themselves, 'Will our readers in Kensington understand this?' As long as it is asked in the interests of
clarity rather than in the spirit of meanness.

'Creative' writers, on the other hand, should occasionally ask themselves, 'Am I writing something
engrossing here, or is it crap?'

The best advice I can give to any would-be writer
is that if you think a word will fox or befuddle a core
of readers, as opposed to the odd one, it's probably
best to look for a simpler word. However, if the
difficult word you chose is the only one that will do
the job ... use it.

As someone who has graduated from journalist to
writer of books, I have allowed my vocabulary a freer
rein. I use a more varied and probably rather more
erudite vocabulary. I try to let the words and phrases
flow from brain to page, and then maybe consider if I
have used any inappropriate ones.

As I've said a few hundred times, it will come with
practice.

The tabloid journalist is a much maligned beast these
days (and here I plead guilty to maligning because the
tabloid celebrity culture drives me mad). But tabloid
journalism at its finest – think the *Mirror* of my youth
– is a joy. Simple and expressive. Yes, sensationalist,
too, when it has to be.

I love the front-page manifesto written by Silvester
Bolam, the *Mirror* editor from 1948-53, before I was
old enough to read it. This is an extract:

The Mirror is a sensational paper. We make no

apology for that. We believe in the sensational presentation of news and views, especially important news and views, as a necessary and valuable public service in these days of mass readership and democratic responsibility.

Sensationalism does not mean distorting the truth. It means the vivid and dramatic presentation of events so as to give them a forceful impact on the mind of the reader. It means big headlines, vigorous writing, **SIMPLIFICATION** *into familiar everyday language, and the wide use of illustration by cartoon and photograph ...*

Every great problem facing us – the world economic crisis (not much changed there, then), *diminishing food supplies, the population puzzle, the Iron Curtain and a host of others – will only be understood by the ordinary man busy with his daily tasks if he is hit hard and hit often with the facts ...*

... The Mirror and its millions of readers prefer the vivid to the dull and the vigorous to the timid.

No doubt we make mistakes, but we are at least alive.

Brilliant stuff! Shame it all dumbed down.

I have highlighted but one word. It's a word that should be becoming familiar to you.

SIMPLE WAY WITH PREPOSITIONS
(AND MY APOLOGIES IF THIS IS STARTING
TO GET A BIT TECHNICAL* See footnote)

Yes, prepositions – those little 'at', 'in', 'up' 'with' words – also get a section to themselves, because some people get so wound up about them.

Shame when there's such a simple solution. All you have to do is give the offending construction a little thought, or give yourself a little Rawlins' Area talking-to.

I start by resisting the almost, but not quite, overwhelming desire to repeat Churchill's famous retort on prepositions (look it up if you don't know). But only because it's not as funny as the child's complaint that goes: *'What did you bring that book that I don't like to be read to out of up for?'*

Not only is it funny – it's the perfect put-down for over-zealous grammarians who say you should never, on pain of death, end a sentence with a preposition.

What rubbish. It's perfectly acceptable to end a sentence with a preposition as long as it reads well; be that in your head or out loud.

'What do you need the gun for?' is fine.

'For what do you need the gun?' is tortuous.

However ... beware the preposition that goes awol and pops up just where it likes in the middle of a sentence.

As in: *'The council managed to track the tenant responsible for the damage down before the police.'*

Erm ... down before the police?

Try: *'The council managed to track down the tenant ...'*

Our language is littered with verbs that take on a new meaning when they are followed by a preposition (or an adverb). Let me remind you of just a few of the more commonly used ones, and what can happen when you separate them:

Call off

Nelson called the party for his regular drinking mates from the pub off just before he fell into the harbour.

Sign up

Sir Alex signed the skilful but ageing defender from Ayr up for a pittance.

Give away

The Chancellor gave the secret of his unexpected tax cuts in the Budget away to his talkative taxi driver.

Take down

The editor took the list of prepositions used in stupid or funny ways down before the visitors arrived.

Look how much easier life becomes when you reinstate the errant words immediately after their controlling verbs:

Nelson called off the party for ...

Sir Alex signed up the ageing defender ...

The Chancellor gave away the ...

The editor took down the list ...

That's all there is to it.

Simple enough?

*I have mentioned this more than once already, but it bears repetition for those who still don't quite get it.

All good writers have technical skill. But each has his or her *own* technical skill, acquired, built up, and honed over time.

A great painter doesn't have to think 'pointillism today?' or 'maybe a little impasto' – he just does it instinctively, without thinking; without the need to know what it's called.

I've just had a quick Google – you're never too old for it – and come across some grammatical terms that I don't know the meaning of (nice little preposition ending there).

Apposition? Diaeresis? (I would guess something to do with vowel problems). Ultima?

Perhaps I knew them once; perhaps I was taught them at school and have forgotten them. It matters not a jot.

However … to explain some things I just *have* to use the odd technical term. I'm keeping it as simple as possible, in the belief that most people will know roughly what a preposition or a participle is. Or will at least have heard the terms.

If you have just learnt a new one, so be it.

I won't mind if you forget it immediately.

SIMPLE FINISH

Sorry, all you people who can't stand football, but after all that scholarly art stuff, it has to be done.

Piddletrenthide Reserves have been practising hard and have pieced together some good passing moves. But they can't seem to get the finish quite right. They over-elaborate and miss the easy chance; or get anxious and snatch at the chance. Either way, the ball ends up wide of the mark.

And so it often is with the novice reporter.

Here's the scenario: the news editor has given him or her a press release, requesting 'maybe a hundred or so words, or more if it's worth it'.

This new, hermaphrodite reporter (who I will now f-emasculate for simplicity's sake) just loves writing; loves to demonstrate a skill that he is now *getting paid for*! Yes, it's now a profession, and he has to demonstrate that he is worthy of the calling.

So he squeezes every last morsel out of the press release. Before he knows it, it's 200 words long and begging for mercy; if only he could see it.

Come Thursday, publication day, he discovers that the editor has reduced his masterpiece to two paragraphs totalling 53 words. The bastard!

But this is no timid tyro. He girds his lions, realises his mistake and sorts out his loins, and bravely asks the editor why she chopped his masterpiece down to virtually nothing.

But this is no uncaring tyrant. She explains sympathetically that she had lots more important stories to squeeze in this week. She smiles benignly and adds, 'Besides, do you really think the town wants to know that the new scout headquarters has a special knot-tying demonstration area? And that the bouquet the Mayoress was given after the opening ceremony contained freesias as well as daffs. And that the County Scout Leader couldn't make it because of a hospital appointment ...'

Oh, bugger!

A harsh lesson but hopefully soon learned.

Think you've got it? Let's try to make sure; it could save a lot of blushes one day.

As the newest recruit to *The London Evening*, you are left in the office while the rest of the reporting staff are out chasing up some sort of bus crash, to fill up a special late edition, with new front and back pages, and as much of pages 2 and 3 as necessary.

The nice news editor, who you fancy like mad even though she is ten years your senior, directs you to the online *History of The Hedera*.

'We need some background for inside,' she says with an encouraging smile. 'Just pick out the best bits for a potted history, please.'

This is the gist of it:

'The building housing the current incarnation of THE HEDERA comprised of three seperate offices – an insurance brokerage, an accountancy, and a firm of solicitor's – until 1966.

The year of England's World Cup win was also the year that a little-known French chef, M Jacques Anapes, bought the middle premises. He opened a small Anglo-French café, LA BELLE, that did reasonably well serving the areas office clientele at lunchtime and early evening.

The business was sold on his death two years later, and then changed hands several times before Eric Stash bought it along with the neighbouring office (the solicitors) and transformed the café into a restaurant.

THE HEDERA first came to prominence when Diana Dors, the 'blond bombshell' Actress lunched here. Adam Faith, the Singer became a regular. Many Stars of Stage and Film now dine here.

One such celebrity, the Poet John Betjeman researched the building for a Television Documentary Program, and discovered that it was originally part of a Charnel House (the current kitchen) and a boot-blacking factory (main dining area) in Dickensian London.

In 1990 ...'

Okay, that will do.

So, what do you think? Three separate offices, a pretend French café, passing reference to the World Cup, office clientele ...

That's right – a big 'so what!?'

But ... John Betjeman, laureate and cultural hero for the common man, a charnel house where human remains were kept, a Dickens' boot-blacking factory – wow! And Diana Dors, former national pin-up with famed pneumatic bosom – double wow!

Now we're talking. Even Adam Faith was an interesting character – a pop singer who was bright enough to become a financial journalist and then went bankrupt.

Get writing!

It might be that the news editor, who now reminds you of Diana Dors, asks for more than even that little treasure trove warrants. If so, that is the time to go back to The Hedera's beginnings. Tack it on the end. The subeditors can easily lop it from there.

By keeping everything tight and sharp, as well as simple, you will be doing everybody a favour: the subeditors because your copy will be a joy to handle; the editor because the current edition will be on time and highly readable; and you because your stock will rise every time you slot home this goal.

I am not going to give you my version this time – but I'll be around eventually to check your efforts. You have been warned.

I would, however, as is my wont, like to point out a few things the alert reporter should have spotted in the online piece:

* *'Comprised **of**'* is one word too many. *Comprise* does not take the *of*.

* *'Seperate'*? Shoot the spell checker!

*'*Firm of solicitor's*.' Solicitor's what? And was there just the one? If you missed the mistake, go back to Apostrophes in part one of the primer.

* *'Areas office clientele.'* How many areas? This time an apostrophe has been missed out.

* *'**Blond** bombshell?'* Miss Dors was all woman, and thus a ***blonde** bombshell*.

*Why do an Actress, a Singer, Stars of Stage and Film, Poet, and Television Documentary warrant capital letters? Quite ...

*And the computerised *Program* will – in my book – never replace the English *programme* for a TV show, let alone start with a capital P.

* *'Diana Dors, the 'blond bombshell' Actress lunched there ...'* and similar following descriptions are all missing a second comma, as in: *'Diana Dors, the 'blonde bombshell' actress, lunched there ...'*

*The charnel house appears to be lumped in with Dickens but was, of course, much earlier.

That's it. Except to say that those of you young enough to query the spelling of Dors might like to know that the delightful Diana was born Diana Mary Fluck.

The name change followed a request by film producers after she won her first major part. She said later: "I suppose they were afraid that if my real name was in lights and one of the lights blew ..."

Sorry, Flucks everywhere. Couldn't resist it.

COMPLICATIONS OF CREATION

I can hear it now: those readers more interested in 'creative' writing – be it books, plays, films, poetry, copywriting – scratching their collective head.

Short, concise, simple? No reaching out to anything peripheral? No flights of fantasy? No transports of delight, or fear, or deep thought? Sounds like a strait-jacket.

They have a good point. It *is* enforced discipline, be it enforced by an avenging outside agency (the editor) or by oneself. But it is discipline of the highest order. For the best of reasons.

Discipline and ever-increasing experience (plus a modicum of flair, of course) will eventually tell you when you can deviate from the main thrust; when your tangent has gone far enough; when you have used enough semicolons.

And here I must briefly go off on my own tangent. Enough semicolons? Enough examples? Enough clever descriptions? Those three question marks will do nicely. The golden Rule Of Three, which can apply to many activities, works nearly every time in writing. Look back through my little primer and you will find many examples. Occasionally I might stray to four (possibly more when the moon turns blue), but only if it improves the narrative, the flow, the overall read. And there's another little threesome.

Anyway … back to the main thrust.

Keep *everything* simple? I can hear the doubters

ask. Okay, so you've highlighted Hemingway, but what's simple about, say, Mailer or Miller? Or Shakespeare?

Well ... Norman Mailer had a reputation for complex, extravagant sentences, but many say his best book was the much simpler *The Executioner's Song*, the story based on the life of murderer Gary Gilmore, who demanded his stayed execution be carried out.

Henry Miller weaves short and simple sentences with long and dense sentences into arcane passages that the less scholarly (including me and probably most of my acquaintances) have to read twice. And he married five times. His namesake Arthur, the playwright, had the obligatory golden Rule of Three Wives, but then one of them *was* Marilyn Monroe. Who, for very young readers, was the veritable full-bodied Hollywood version of Diana Dors.

Mailer beat both Millers by totting up six wives.

Shakespeare, on the other hand, had just the one wife, but he did leave her his second-best bed in his will, and the rest of the world a legacy that might never be bettered.

So many of his best lines have become ingrained in the everyday that it's easy to flip from one to the next without giving a thought to their provenance. And spoken English has changed so much since he was dashing off these masterpieces in the sixteenth century that every generation finds it a little harder to follow than the previous generation.

So, creative writers ... I have gone off at all sorts

of tangents in the page you have just read. Did you follow them? Or did I befuddle you?

Norman Mailer, two Millers, Gary Gilmore, lots of wives, Marilyn Monroe, more Dors, Shakespeare and his bed.

Just what are Monroe and Dors doing in there?

Spicing up proceedings a tad? Entertaining the non-academic reader? Bolstering the word count?

No, not necessarily any of those things. They are merely the result of a lack of planning and/or thought.

As I said in part one, there are basically two ways to approach a story: plan every last detail, or let the characters or events take you where they will. But if it's the latter, you need to be just as disciplined.

You need to read and check every episode. Have you overdone or undercooked the detail? Have you let it dribble on to boredom? Is there *any* connection with the main thrust? Does it add or detract from the overall enjoyment of the read?

This is when you really need to know when to stop and what to leave out. It's a discipline, like every other, that comes with time and practice. And there's probably no better place to learn it than in the front line of journalism.

A book, or indeed a news story, needs to be as long as it needs to be.

As Shakespeare put it: This is the short and the long of it *(The Merry Wives Of Windsor, 1600)*.

Just before I depart the subject of 'creative' writing, I can imagine that those of you who want to write books, rather than newspaper/magazine stories, are moaning that not enough of my little primer has been devoted to the art you aspire to.

On the face of it, you appear to be right. 'Creative' writing has taken the back seat.

But ... writing is writing. And it is all creative in its own way. If you are to be any good at it, you will be able to turn your hand to almost anything: articles, short stories, novels, plays, film and TV scripts.

And if you have learnt the basics and the disciplines of the newsroom – with a little help from a little primer – you will eventually be able to do just that.

Twain, Dickens, Mailer, both the Millers, Hemingway, Daniel Defoe, Samuel Taylor Coleridge, George Orwell, Graham Greene, and Bill Bryson – to name but eleven who could give Piddletrenthide Reserves a run for their money – all wrote for newspapers.

(I must apologise to my female readers if all this seems a smidge male-heavy, but I'm only just catching up with women's football.)

THE COMPLICATED NEWS STORY

There are, by their very nature, some stories that are complicated beyond basic comprehension. Financial news perhaps; council or government announcements involving lots of different people, companies, regulations, and time references, for instance. And they have to be told as simply as your vocabulary and grasp of the subject allow.

Not easy if it's something like the following few paragraphs, tucked away in council minutes of a subcommittee meeting. A meeting that the council admin office totally forgot when it was sending out its monthly meetings schedule to the local press.

Now, concentrate:

The Borough Council recommends that, in light of the planning decisions left pending from the Borough Local Plan 2001 (following represent-ations from TH Restaurants), the original statute of 1966, agreed by the then leaseholder, be invoked. Therefore, the premises at 22 Calamity Street will revert to office accommodation.

Mr Jacques Anapes agreed on 30th of July, 1966 to amend the lease to require transfer of the premises to the Borough Council if the leaseholder or lessees were unable to continue business in the premises.

The Borough Council Chief Executive Officer, B. Rhodes, has, therefore, signed the order to authorise the purchase of the appropriate deeds.

The current joint lessees, that is TH Restaurants, the Managing Director of TH Restaurants, E.C. Stash, and TH Restaurants Company Secretary, Mrs Z. Stash, have appealed the decision.

The Borough Council Leader, Councillor E.V.N. Sakes, has requested the Borough Chief Planning Officer, E. L. Wistie, to put the rebuilding of the premises out to tender.

In light of the incident of January 21, 2013, the Borough Council has instructed the Health And Safety Executive to investigate all aspects of the business housed at the Calamity Street address.

They have also been requested to advise on the suitability of the premises, and the car park to the rear, for Borough administration purposes.

It might take a couple of reads before you realise that the borough council has used the unplanned demolition of The Hedera restaurant to compulsory purchase (no doubt at an appropriate knock-down price) the prime plot of land. And not only that, the conniving burghers want the prime spot for themselves. Well, it's near the tube, close to the shops and little eateries where busy officials can nip out for a quick snack.

So there you go, would-be reporter. You know what to do next, don't you?

Of course.

Call Mr Sakes and/or Mr Wistie (Mr Rhodes is bound to be far too busy) – or better still, see them face to face – and ask them precisely what the minutes mean. And if they bluster and prevaricate, spell out what *you* think they mean, and ask them if you are right.

This time I won't trouble you with my own version of the story. I said most of it in the paragraph after the italics. But it might benefit you to have a go. I can wait.

Finished? Good.

I would just add that, for the would-be journalist, this little primer is about writing your story, and not about the ins and outs of getting your story. That's a whole different skill, and one that you will soon learn on the job (and if you don't, you will soon be looking for another career).

The purpose of this little chapter is to demonstrate that the world of officialdom and business is often quite happy to embrace the *complicated*; *simple* is far too easy for the rest of the world to follow.

So you must learn to spot and decipher *complicated;* you must learn to turn it into *simple.*

Not only is it improving your skills, and ensuring that your reader doesn't give up and go for a pint. But it is also helping to keep the pettifoggers in check, and that's a good enough reason on its own to embrace the *simple*.

Time for another little break.

FINAL DO'S AND DON'TS

You will, of course, come across other do's and don'ts in your new career, and hopefully you will have the nous to add them to your own list. I am merely pointing out the most common, the most insidious, and the most annoying to discerning readers.

ACTOR
Use for both sexes (unless dealing with award for best actress). As with singer, artist, comedian, writer, it describes the subject's occupation, not gender.

AGEING
Aging is a dictionary alternative, but looks like an oriental spice.

AWOL
The armed forces' old Absent WithOut Leave, but now sufficiently entrenched to be the lower-case awol.

BORNE (OUT)
The past participle of bear (out) – as in *borne out by the facts*. But *born out of necessity.*

BURNED or BURNT?
Or, indeed, dreamed or dreamt, leaned or leant, leaped or leapt, learned or learnt, smelled or smelt; spelled or spelt?

Tricky chaps; different newspapers come up with

different decisions. Basically, they are interchangeable, although the British preference is usually *–t*, while Americans go for *–ed*.

To be consistent, try this: burned is the 'active' past tense, as in *Alfred burned the cakes*; burnt is the 'adjectival' participle, as in *the unwatched cakes were burnt*.

A wordsmith I respect swears by: *I learned,* but *I have learnt*.

CHORDS
Are musical. Cords are vocal

COLON
Use a colon, rather than a semicolon, where the second part of the sentence defines the first part (in a list, for example). *He had three reasons not to go: it was a full moon, it was cold, and the host was an idiot.*

DO'S AND DON'TS
Yes, even sticklers' rules have their exceptions. *Do's and don'ts* is my personal compromise on needless apostrophes.

The *dos* in the strictly correct *dos and don'ts* looks like a computer operating system, but complying to the logic of the alternative, *do's and don't's* looks like an apostrophe fest.

ELLIPSIS (plural, ellipses)
Just the three dots, please (new writers often go for the full epidemic), and use a space before and after the

dots, but no extra full point if it's at the end of a sentence. As in, *Perhaps Mr Clegg would never understand ...*

FAMOUS

If something or someone is famous, there is no need to say so. 'The famous footballer David Beckham'? Give your readers credit.

FARTHER

Indicates distance. Further means additional.

FOLLOWING

Silly overused word where time is involved. The simple *after* flows and reads much better.

HANGED

People are hanged (yes, even in the 21st century). Pictures are hung.

INFAMOUS

What, like Jack the Ripper? Get away. See *Famous.*

INTO (and the vagaries of ONTO)

Not always one word – work it out before you write it. *Mr Obama walked into a fire hydrant*, but *Mr Obama went in to dinner.*

Onto is one for the pedants to fight over. But, more often than not, two words seems right, looks right, and is right. As in, *Mr Obama passed the news on to his aides.*

LAY and LIE

Sorry ... but remember 'transitive' and 'intransitive' from school/college? This is where you need them. A transitive verb needs an object (*David kicked Nick*); an intransitive verb doesn't (*David hyperventilated*).

So ... lay (past tense, laid) is a transitive verb. You *lay a carpet* (past tense, *laid the carpet*). Lie (past tense, lay; past participle, lain) is an intransitive verb. You *lie flat on the floor* (past tense, *lay on the floor last night*; past participle, *the floor where you had lain*).

Piece of cake.

LIKE, SUCH AS

Use *like* as a comparison with a specific noun, as in *he drinks like a publican*. Otherwise it is best to use *such as*. As in, *he preferred to watch the better teams, such as Arsenal, Chelsea, Leicester City ...*

MARSHAL

Has but one 'l', whether it's a noun (as in sheriff) or a verb (as in muster); although marshalling and marshalled have two, but not in the US.

MEET *WITH*!?

No! Don't do it! *Meet* will suffice ...

NO QUESTION ... ARE YOU SURE?

'There was no question that he was lying.' What does that mean – he was lying, or he was telling the truth? It means the latter, but sounds like the former, so try to avoid the construction.

OKAY

Is another Rawlins' aberration. Most style guides go for OK; I much prefer it as a word rather than initials. Okay?

PER ANNUM?

Got a lot of Latin speakers among your readers? 'Premiums of £1,000 *a year*' will do nicely.

PROBE

A probe is something a doctor sticks somewhere you'd rather he didn't. The best word for an investigation is ... investigation. Or maybe inquiry.

ROOFS

Is the plural; not *rooves*.

SAY, SAID

By far the best words for reporting speech. Safe, neutral, never pejorative. And much underrated. Some new writers go to great lengths not to say *say;* presumably because someone has told them to avoid repetition. So instead, their characters *exclaim*, *assert*, *disclose*, and once in a while *ejaculate* (which always makes me come over all unnecessary).

SPEAKING OF WHICH ...

People do not talk in abbreviations or figures, so spell them out when reporting speech.

The nurse said, 'Dr Kildare saw 22 patients yesterday' has two mistakes.

It should read: *The nurse said, '**Doctor** Kildare saw **twenty-two** patients yesterday.'*

Some newspapers would have no qualms about using 22 in reported speech, and that's their affair, but never in a book, please.

TRAGIC
Fatal accidents are always tragic; it doesn't need spelling out.

WARD OR WARDS?
Upward, downward, backward do not take an 's' when used as adjectives, as in *downward slope*. But when used as adverbs, add the 's', as in *looking downwards*.

BEYOND DESCRIPTION

There is one part of the wordsmith's art that does not come naturally or easily to me; and, I suspect, to quite a few others brought up in the newsroom. And that is the deeper reaches of descriptive writing.

The reporter and subeditor learn to relate the latest news in the leanest, tautest manner, often under the pressure of a fast-approaching deadline.

The main event (the crash, the fire, the scandal) is all: the protagonists, names, ages, other relevant personal details, where, when, why, how, reaction, quotes, both sides, balance, immediacy. Get it in!

There is, or can be, a certain amount of descriptive writing in feature articles, but then again they tend to centre on one specific person or undertaking.

One of my early books had Oxford characters going on holiday in a distant earthly paradise. The first member of my family to read it said the descriptions of the distant earthly paradise brought it to life; whereas Oxford was more any old city than dreaming spires.

He was right, the bastard.

I didn't know the distant earthly paradise, so, unable to afford the time or air fare, I researched it thoroughly (so thoroughly I felt I had been there) and gladly passed on the sights and sounds and feel of the place to my readers; whereas I knew Oxford so well I forgot I had to bother.

Lesson learned. But only up to point. I still tend to

get so involved in my narrative that my descriptions tend to be sketchy rather than artistic or elegant. But now at least I tend to remember, give myself a good talking-to, and see where I can refine sketchy.

I would advise new writers to get in the habit of refining early on, before they get in the habit of barely sketching.

Let's give it a go.

The owners of the demolition site that was The Hedera restaurant have invited *The London Evening* to send a reporter and photographer to look behind the scenes of the scaffolding-and-tarpaulin-enclosed wasteland they want to continue owning.

They have vowed to fight the borough council through the courts to retain ownership in the face of a compulsory purchase order.

The managing director, Eric Stash (reputedly a latter-day Kray), and his wife and company secretary, Zelda Stash, want to meet the press to show them the damage and their plans for rebuilding. And to harangue the borough council for even daring to suggest that the restaurant in any way breached lease or legal safety requirements.

You go, with thoughts of horses' heads and/or council corruption, and are guided through the tarpaulin by the Stashes' barn door of a 'spokesman'.

Introductions are soon made. Eric is suitably squat and saturnine; Zelda is proper moll material. They show you and snapper Jason around the debris, pointing out what to photograph, and then show you their architect's plans for the restoration of The Hedera, which looks precisely like the old Hedera.

'So then, John,' says Eric, 'you know this council guy Rhodes? Chief executive tosser, or whatever he calls hisself.'

You nod.

'Know he uses council cash for backhanders?'

You do a shrug-cum-shake-of-the-head to indicate, No, but if you can prove anything, I'm your journo.

'We have pictures of him and his missus wining and dining the chief fire tosser. No doubt he bribed the fire tosser to say regs was breached. And the health and safety tosser woman. Pardon my French, Zeld.'

'Have you any proof?' you venture.

'Yeah. Show him, Zeld.'

Zelda adjusts her cleavage for Jason's lens as she delves into a capacious Ted Baker handbag and comes out with a handful of postcard-size prints.

They were taken at a barbecue party (in the past week, if the digital camera date is correct). Rhodes is indeed shown talking and shaking hands with several people you seem to recognise. Could be the chief fire officer; could be the local health and safety supremo. Could be just any old barbecue old friends and colleagues have been invited to.

'I'll have to check these out,' you say, tucking the prints into your jacket pocket.

'You do that, John, you do that. Look forward to reading your article. Go, get 'em, boy.'

You smile a sickly smile and indicate to Jason it's

time to go; he has more than enough pictures of Zelda's cleavage.

Okay – you have done all the checks you can reasonably do, and there is little doubt. Eric and Zelda are trying it on.

Yes, the chief tossers were at the barbecue, but it was a private friendly affair at the Rhodes' residence. Although it cannot be entirely ruled out, impropriety is highly unlikely; at least at this gathering (although there is more detective work to be done on the council's compulsory purchase order).

However, there is still a story to be written: you and Jason are the first journalists to be invited behind the tarpaulin; the first journalists to have an interview with the Stashes.

I can tell you that the double-decker has long been dragged out, the front wall demolished, the inner walls left as jagged remnants, half the ceiling caved in, leaving mounds of bricks and plaster, doors and glass, matchwood tables and chairs. A pair of expensive sunglasses caught on an undamaged table top reflect a weak sun.

Please feel free to embellish this (a little) should you wish. Now, using the basic journalistic judgment you have so far garnered, write a piece that combines a powerful description with suspected shenanigans.

Grab some paper, or call up a text page, and write a piece that you and your editor will be proud of. Finish it before you turn the page and compare it with my effort.

If you thought it through, you might have decided that Jason's pictures (if he is as good with landscapes as he is with cleavages) are worth an intro, if not a thousand words. The main one, above your precious words, shows the Stashes surveying the extent of the devastation. An inset picture shows the sunglasses.

So …

This is all that remains of the haven of celebrity that less than a fortnight ago was heaving with the famous and rich.

Piles of rubble, tables and chairs reduced to kindling, a pair of designer sunglasses, an elegant high-heeled shoe, and a bill for £349.85 (including a bottle of fine champagne) mark the spot and the moment of madness that destroyed it.

This is the death scene of The Hedera, the London restaurant where actors and singers gathered to wine and dine away from the madding crowd. Until a week last Wednesday when a hijacked double-decker bus ploughed into a busy lunchtime service.

Six people died; none of them celebrities (the madding crowd could usually book a table up to 7pm). Lady Haha escaped because she was in the loo. Micky Bubble sustained multiple injuries and remains in intensive care. His dining companion, Amanda Kameroon, is recovering from a broken leg and two fractured arms.

(These key facts have to be regurgitated for new readers – never assume that all your readers saw the first instalment – and this seems to be the logical place to put them. A brief paragraph about Desmond Mollyjo could follow.)

The restaurant's owners, Eric and Zelda Stash, showed me (and photographer Jason Canon) round the shattered shell of their business yesterday afternoon.

The two mounds of rubble almost at right angles, towards the back of the room, were all that remained of the alcove where Angelina Holy and Fred Pitt often canoodled.

Two wrecked tables and a hatstand that had become entwined, like some fantastic Antony Gormley sculpture, rose defiantly from the detritus near the window where Kenny Brantub liked to quietly read from Shakespeare.

And then there were the ghosts of The Hedera. I could almost feel their presence as Eric pointed out their framed sepia photos, now but broken memories littering the fallen bricks and plaster. Lord Larry, lovely Jimmy and Tony from Hollywood, Joanie, of course, and Hitch devouring steaks as if on a one-man mission to make the cow extinct.

Eric would smile in memory while Zelda blinked back impending tears; and then Zelda would laugh while Eric bit his bottom lip. Their hearts, minds, and demeanours flitted back and forth, until the future was mentioned. Then they were as one; one steely determination to rebuild their beloved Hedera.

And there lies another story. The borough council has ruled that ...

So there you have it. It's not fine literature. It's not belle-lettre. And it's far from the finest journalism ever to pass over my desk. But it's not crap, either. It's not mediocre or merely acceptable.

It's good. It flows, it engages the reader. It conjures up pictures (to complement Jason's efforts), and that is what I was aiming for.

I would go so far as to say that, for a piece written at one short sitting, I'm very pleased with it.

I hope you are equally pleased with your effort.

LOSING BATTLE WARRIORS

I must wrap up this little primer with a final word about my losing battle warriors stalking the pages of parts one and two in the never-ending fight to save the English language from philistines (just one LBW in part three as I concentrate on other matters).

I can hear the world of non-warriors asking, If it's a losing battle, what is the point of fighting it?

Bear with me. Battles will be lost; the world will move on. And probably quite rapidly. Using nouns as verbs will oldhat not only the baby boomers' grandchildren but possibly also the baby boomers' children themselves who are inventing this rubbish.

But let's try to think it through more carefully.

All this rubbish stems from ignorance or wilful dumbing-down. Some thicko starts saying *'myself'* instead of *'me'* because he or she doesn't know any better. The thicko next-door hears it and supposes it to be correct because it sounds vaguely official (yes, that's the way officials learned to write, and now talk). And before you know it, the contagion has spread to that huge part of the population that thinks reality TV is real life.

So the point is: if we don't put up decent defences, the world and its grandchildren will be swamped by the tide of ignorance.

So the next point is: those people who have stuck a finger in the dyke have made some reparation. The Plain English Campaign has signed up many local authorities and major businesses to fight the good fight. The various guides to plain English are trying to make headway in our schools and colleges.

So the final point for writers is: we are in the front line. Millions of people who will never bother to consult the Plain English Campaign or the various guides, do read newspapers, magazines, and books.

Those that are well-written, and many are, are demonstrating every day how language should be used. And now it's your turn.

You are practising daily; you are improving daily.

So welcome to the front line. Pull up a gun carriage. The battle may not be lost yet ...

THE BATTLE WE MUST NEVER LOSE

Finally, before I sign off, I think it behoves me as a long-time journalist, and upholder of the faith, to say a few words about the other battle for the British press.

It stems from the scandal of the phone hacking perpetrated by a handful of bastards from the lower reaches of the tabloid spectrum.

Lord Justice Leveson was asked to hold a wide-ranging inquiry into press behaviour and report back with recommendations for the government.

He did so as 2012 drew to a close, recommending 'voluntary independent self-regulation' for the press, with a 'statutory underpinning'.

Oh dear …

FREE PRESS, FREE SPEECH

Yes, it's a simple as that. Muzzle the press and the shysters have a field day.

Everyone I know in the business deplores the antics of those few unscrupulous hacks who hacked the phones of celebrities, royalty, politicians, and even a young murder victim.

There is even sympathy for some of the celebrities whose fame owes much to the press, who court the press for publicity, who thrive in the public glare, and then scream as soon as one word of censure appears.

But there is none for the pressure groups who saw the Leveson report as a chance to further their own causes – and stuff free speech.

I owe a debt to superb contemporaneous reports by Andrew Gilligan in *The Sunday Telegraph* for the following information:

The Royal College of Psychiatrists wanted the Leveson report to call for an end to 'sensationalising' crime reports because it impeded the 'rehabilitation of the perpetrators'. An Islamic lobby group called Engage (whose members have defended extremists and even the killing of British soldiers) wanted an end to 'discriminatory' reporting against Muslims. The self-styled Youth Media Agency said 'negative' media coverage of young people 'harmed their aspirations'.

Lord Justice Leveson accepted these grievances in full; with a vague nod to giving these sorts of groups scope to add 'balance' to any report.

What this could possibly boil down to, in the ultimate scenario, is a pressure group having the power to hold up or hold off a story casting any serious aspersions on their particular sacred cows. And, in effect, anyone under investigation would be entitled to see anything a journalist has written about them. And then seek to have it edited or expunged.

They would also be entitled to see a journalist's notes and discover his or her sources. This means that no journalist would be able to promise confidentiality to whistleblowers – or, as I prefer to call them, those few brave people prepared to speak out against incompetence, injustice and corruption. And no confidentiality would mean no whistleblowers.

What utter nonsense. Is this what the pro-Levesons want: a system that lets injustice run riot?

A free press *needs* to be partial. To have the freedom to investigate wrong-doing, immorality, political correctness gone mad.

Of course, responsible journalists ask the subjects of any investigation to offer their side of the story, and then give it due airing, but a free press does not kowtow to demands to pull a story.

If that sort of power were enshrined in law, MPs would still be fiddling their expenses, Stafford Hospital would still be killing by neglect, and god knows what bankers would be up to.

'Independent self-regulation' is, of course, a contradiction in terms.

And validation by the state is the first step to state-controlled media. Corruption, nepotism, and intolerance run riot. It ain't on, is it?

As I write, a coalition government has opted for a compromise involving a Royal Charter. This would allow an 'independent regulator' to dictate matters such as the form, placement, and size of an apology by an errant newspaper.

Spot the not-so-thin end of the wedge?

I fear it could be some time before a Royal Charter allows the public to dictate the abjectness of an apology by a government minister responsible for the next billion-pound foul-up; or the degree of abasement by the next criminal MP to bring parliament, hence the country, hence you and me, into disrepute.

It could possibly be even longer, I suspect, before film buffs can rely on a Royal Charter requiring one-trick actors to apologise for yet another bumbling-Englishman performance.

Yeah, I know – cheap shot. But sometimes you just have to hammer home the point, no matter how bluntly. I don't want so-called celebrities, other unelected nonentities, and assorted anonymous donors deciding how the press should or shouldn't do its vital work. Do you?

Democracy depends on a free press that can make whatever shots are required for the common good.

So please take up the baton. Be prepared to wield it against the naysayers.

They will keep trying.

NOW THEN ... GENIUSES

As I said at the start of Part 3 ... undisputed geniuses. Da Vinci, Michelangelo, Shakespeare, Beethoven, Mozart, Bach, Darwin, Newton, Einstein, Faraday, Edison.

But geniuses in one lifetime? Say, mine? Picasso, Hawking, Churchill, Berners-Lee, Groening, Matt (the *Telegraph* cartoonist), Woody Allen ... and it's already starting to get a mite subjective.

Confining myself to *literary* genius in the 20th and 21st centuries, I have already mentioned several in earlier chapters. I could add Wilde (just scraped in at 1900), Wodehouse, Shaw, Kipling, Salinger, Harper Lee, Laurie Lee, and loads more.

They may not be quite in the Da Vinci class, but who is? There are sparks of genius, if not flares and flames, in so many writers. And we all love different sparks. Say, Steinbeck, Wells, Woolf, Austen, all three Brontës, Grisham, King, Bryson, Mantel, Douglas Adams. A line-up guaranteed to whip the arse off Piddletrenthide Reserves – even with six female players this time (with Mantel as sub, I fancy).

Read as many as you can. Absorb them. Try to figure out how they do it. But don't try to copy them.

Read and write. Then read and write some more. Practise. Write a poem, write a short story, write a novel if you have the stamina.

One day someone might spot *your* spark and nod. Maybe smile that certain smile that a spark can generate.

Printed in Great Britain
by Amazon